# Light and Stone

*Essays on Writing*
*and the*
*Realities of Publishing*

## T.E.Watson

HIGHLANDS PRESS

Publisher -Highlands Press an imprint of
Heather and Highlands Publishing
United States of America.

ISBN (13) 978-1-58478-063-2
ISBN (10) 1-58478-063-0
BISAC - Language Arts & Disciplines / Authorship
Library of Congress Control Number: 2017908234
Highland Press, Paradise, CA

Light and Stone is a compilation of writing tips, suggestions
and methods, including philosophical essays from the
author's 43 plus years in the publishing industry.
Self Help- Writing, How to, Publishing.
Printed in the United States of America / First Edition

# Contents

# Contents

# Introduction

Light and Stone was a request by an agent friend in Massachusetts. He asked me if at some point I ever decided to write a book on writing that I should let them know. That was some time ago, and I have decided to take on this task. I have found it both enlightening and entertaining. *Light and Stone* has turned out to be one of my most requested works.

*Light and Stone* is a book of essays, shorts about writing, portions of the journey of one writer, and the experiences therein. It is ideas and opinions. It is thoughts and suggestions for possible would-be authors. These are most definitely works for new and experienced writers. Yes, many writers in the world are most willing to share their thoughts.
I would like to share these experiences with you.
Some will be discouraging though not demeaning. Many will be encouraging. Some items and topics will help you on your path to success.

Some items will bring out your creative side, and there will be subjects that will make you think and evaluate the reasons you want to become a writer or full-fledged author.

They are pertinent to your journey to publication. You will notice when you read this, your increased understanding of the writing process, or it may make you question because you don't agree with what it states. That is fine. If I did do that, then I have done my job. I have made you think and feel. That is the goal of every writer and author.

There are times when every would-be author wants to have instant gratification. I can tell you that does not happen. The so-called overnight successes are false. They do not exist. Every writer, every creative person wants that, but when they are honest with themselves, it is an artificial fantasy. This book will help you understand the path you must travel to get to some meaning of success.

There will come a time when your idea of success becomes reachable, and yet, you will see you are so close and so far away at the same time, it becomes exasperating and frustrating. So much so, it feels as if you will never make it.

Don't give up. Keep reading. Turn the page. Visualize and imagine the world where you are a writer that is helping the universe become a better place.

The author who, through their words, can explain how to obtain that better place and possibly generate further inspiration is always a success.

Every journey starts with the first step. Take that step or stand still. If a little work causes your willingness to freeze solid where you currently stand, then authorship is not for you. Reality can either kick you in the pants or sit on you, never allowing you to move.
Only you can decide. The ball is in your court now. It's up to you.

Mark Twain once said, "If you want to be a writer, write!"

That's all well and good but if you want to become a published author. You know, one of those few of us that get paid for our thoughts. You should have someone in your corner, a mentor who helps you through the ropes

A coach for the potentially successful aspiring writer is one you should pay close attention. There are not many of them who know how to help or will help at all. But, whether your job is being a lawyer, a doctor, a kindergarten teacher, or the mother of two, even an executive in the corporate business world, or a manager for some major firm, there is still a desire to see your creative side in print.

It never ceases to amaze me how many professional people would rather be writers than how they are presently making a living.

You may already know, writing is hard, writing is disappointing, and writing is having to deal with negativity all around you. The odds are definitely against you and getting your work published approximately 350,000 to 1.

Are you discouraged yet?

There are definite differences between those who enjoy placing thoughts on paper and those who are dead serious about putting the hours and weeks in, polishing and re-writing, and doing it all over if need be. In the beginning there is no such thing as a successful first draft. It is true with writing as well as writers. Get it into your head now. If you are to be successful, you will work for it without question.

You have gotten over the first hurdle. Now take a breath and leap over the next one.

# About the Cover

During the production of this book *Light and Stone,* some of the people involved in its build have asked why the photo of the almost lightless stone stairway headed upward to the top of, in this case, an actual medieval tower in Scotland. More so the Wallace Monument in Stirling.

I told them this.

The reason for the concept of this castle stairway was simple. It represents the upward climb most writers and authors travel to get to the top of their writers journey. The stone displays the hard climb and the often long one. It also represents the often dark pathway a new writer must travel without any guide whatsoever.

All this to get to the top. Yes, it is a hard step by step trip, but if you stay the course and keep going upward, each step becomes less daunting and the confidence you gain grows helping you to attain your writing goal, whatever that goal may be.

Writing is hard dedicated work. It takes mental strength as well as physical. Lots of it. There are many hard steps on this uphill climb. It is a learning process to make your work as best as it can, but it forces you to always look up to the light. And when you get to the top and are immersed in the light, you can look out over the horizon and gather in your mind all you see.

That is what this cover is about.

T.E.Watson FSA scot

# ABOUT THE COVER

*Part 1–*

# *Light*

# Chapter 1- Starting Out

To begin with, keep at it! Ignore all those who tell you to quit; you'll never make it. All writers have been told many times by others, stop what you are doing, you're wasting your time.

Writers are individuals that hang out with artistic low-lifes in coffee houses. They stereotypically wear dark colored clothing, and corduroy jackets with patches on the elbows and speak of radical ideas of all kinds. Not to mention the dark sunglasses.

Kidding aside, even though that was the stereotypical part of the 50s and early 60s and even part of the 70s. Writers are not like that today.

Yes, some have radical ideas, and yes, some have not so radical ideas, the ideas have been passed around before, but writing is writing, and the process is the same.

However, I have never hung out in a coffee shop or with radical idea slingers.

Being almost prophetic in earlier comments, I already owned a tweed jacket with patches on the elbows, so I took that as a positive thing.

It is not a requirement for becoming a writer, only to, maybe, appear as one.
I would've never gotten where I am today if I paid attention to the naysayers.

Every time anyone told you to stop wasting your time, that should make you more determined to prove them wrong.

There will be those who want to tell you there's no way you can do it. There's absolutely no way you will be successful. You have no talent. You don't know how to write, and there's just no way you're going to make it. The only reason they can tell you this is because they have no idea what they are talking about.

You are among an incredible group of people who have fantastic ideas and who have decided to place those ideas into books and magazines and out into the eyes of the public. Never pay attention to the people who say you cannot do this.

It is only because you have thought about the fear of having somebody tell you, you cannot do it, is the reason you will make it. That is, if you do not give up entirely

after too much thinking on the process.
Over-thinking will make your writing less appealing to read and more difficult to write.

The idea of sticking to what you believe in is simply this. When a writer has an assignment, or is writing freelance work, or is taking on a novel of their own, whatever it is, time becomes your worst enemy. Time becomes the one big thing, always in the window, staring at you.

After a while, it begins to nag and make jeering noises in your direction. All this grinds at your creativity, and your attention becomes distracted toward it, and you are then a victim of time. I have only one thing to suggest.

KNOCK IT OFF!

Your focus needs to readjust and re-tune and then rejuvenate into the area of the paper you were writing.

You only have a short time to produce this work, whatever it is. Your focus is vital to the success of the work. You must change your thought process.
Your mindset and the way you exercise it is up to you.

However, the amount of focus put into your work and the time you are using to make the work happen is a deal you need to strike with the schedule you keep on a daily basis.

The plan you have set forth to use for writing time is essential. It is vital that your plan is followed. Only a short few minutes every day is all one needs to be able to keep on track. All of it takes time.

Concentration and focus are brother and sister. They are hand in hand. This relationship does not always occur. Just as any family member would behave, they do not always get along. Life happens. The same is so when writing.

Remember back when you were in grade school, and your teacher gave an assignment on a Monday, with full expectation that the task be completed, done with punctuation and spelling and all, and turned in the next Friday.

Now, remember your eyes leaving their sockets in fear and exasperation, and a little panic. The thinking was not an issue here. There was no time to think about it. The assignment was simply supposed to be done and turned in on Friday, or perhaps as soon as Thursday.

Your forehead began to sweat, and IT MEANT NOT HAVING ANY FUN AT ALL! AUGGGGHHHH! (echo type sound effect here)

But wait, maybe not.

Perhaps if you were to schedule your time, and figure a way to give time to all these things you are worried about, maybe this time thing would work out after all.

What if all the hubbub and hoopla about constructing a work schedule was correct?

What if you could design a plan that worked?
Think, just for a moment. Will you give yourself that much time each day until you have the assignment done? Here is a different concept, give yourself permission to succeed.

Remember how you felt when you didn't give yourself permission? Did you feel good or did you question the feeling? Did you doubt you could accomplish anything by doing that?

Many years ago I had a basketball coach who always went by this simple strategy regarding shooting, "If you only *think* you have a shot, don't take it. However, if you *know* you have the shot, shoot."

It is true with writing as well. Writing does not always come forth in great sentences to be remembered by the reading masses. Sometimes it is good, some are great, a lot of it is garbage.

But that is why the invention of rewrites happened. If you know you have the story, and it is tight and ready to roll, then put it to paper. It will not be perfect, but it will be a good start. If you have no clue where you are going with your writing, then wait, you will miss the mark.

Timing is everything. Percolate on your writing or what will become your writing. Let it cook and simmer in your mind and then put it to paper and the words will come through easily. However, never forget to put the words down when they are clear enough to place onto paper. Scheduling writing is a form of time allocation. It is keeping a loyal and faithful connection to your work. This verbal child you are raising on paper depends on you to be able to rear it, take care of it, be sure it can and does have the ability to take care of itself in the real world when you release it out into the public eye.

You should construct a writing schedule for your work. Take the time to develop a disciplined writing relationship with your schedule.

Stay with the work to the end, then, even through all the re-writes, despite the frustration level you will reach, all the while staying faithful to that schedule, letting nothing get in your way, you will be successful.

Your schedule is yours to discover. You are the only one that can best realize the part of the day you can do this. Take it by the horns and go for it. Write it down and place it in front of you somewhere it is visible and easy to reference.

But before you write any words, the first thing to write is your schedule. Stick to it with no excuses.

# Chapter 2-
# Beginning at the Beginning

American humorist and author Mark Twain (a.k.a Samuel L. Clemens) was asked how someone might get started in the writing business. He said, "If you want to be a writer, write!"
Makes sense.

When becoming a writer, there are many situations you must accept. One is that you must begin at the beginning. You cannot start in the middle. You will have missed many things you need to know.

Early on is when you must learn and accept that your ego is your worst enemy. It could bring forth feelings of cursing the editor who rejected your work, making you look like a rookie amateur.

You're not alone. Every new writer has felt the same way at one time or another. The idea behind writing is you feel you have something that is so overwhelmingly wonderful, you have to share it. This idea, while you are shaping your writing, is to make your work appear as professional as you can make it. You need to do this especially if you were planning to take on the most challenging genre, writing for children.

The prospect of writing for children is so vast that only those who feel they can indeed persevere and persist will ever get close enough to becoming successful. Giving up at any point would be almost shameful and a real waste of the time it takes to become successful even for just one book.

So why become a children's writer? In the year 2004, there was an approximate number of 8,000 to 12,000 new children's books published worldwide. Not very many compared to today's numbers. That reflects only the new books of medium to large traditional publishers.

This number does not reflect the actual numbers that were submitted, nor does it indicate those who might have made it past the second or third level of editorial review.

Neither does it reflect the market or the actual printed numbers overseas, where a huge majority of books are printed and manufactured. Not to mention those that did not get past rejection letter stage and round file.

Yes, some do get thrown into the rubbish bin. It also does not tell the numbers for any self-published projects, or any books based on a subscription basis. The way you decide to work is up to you. Each demand time and effort.

Now that you've read this, do you know what you are doing, and why you have decided to take on the most difficult topic in literature ?

Ask anyone in the industry, and they will tell you it can become very detrimental to one's confidence and self-esteem. Children's writing is the hardest, the most trying, and the most rejected genre you can undertake. Children's writing must be nothing short of perfect in the way it is written.

It is also the most heavily and severely criticized. You must have a strong sense of self and a ton of knowledge on the topic you are writing for kids. It will clearly show if you don't.

They're asking how do you get started? Or the better question is, where do I start?

First, you've already begun to read and research writer information books; otherwise, you would not be here reading this.

Second, read everything. Even books you would not normally like to read. Take for instance this example. If you were taking piano lessons, your instructor would demonstrate arpeggios and scales, even teacher arrangements that they know.

They will show how to study and practice what they have taught you for that week. If you want to play like Bach, you study Bach's methods and styles. It goes for the rest of those who you wish to emulate.

The same applies to children's writing. Begin with the greats of children's literature. For instance, H.G. Wells, Roald Dahl, Beatrix Potter, and Charles Dickens. These are just a few examples.

Every great writer reads!

Choose your favorites and remember your childhood. Your memory will be your biggest asset as a writer of children's literature. It's been completely worth it. In my years of writing everything from news reports to magazine articles to political and environmental pieces, I still find writing for children the most satisfying. It makes you a stronger writer.

The book *The Natural History of Make-Believe, A Guide to Principal Works of Britain, Europe, and America by John Goldthwaite.* The latest edition published in 1996, gives the history of the children's book as a literary genre and the histories of the authors who wrote these great works.

The beginnings of the children's book or the children's storybook go back as far as the early 1600s and possibly earlier. The evolution of this genre has taken place during a slow and methodical history, starting out as a way for children to be kept quiet by their nannies to the present day thought in which children should be learning to read and to some point entertained with reading. It is a good theory and should be kept as such.

The Harry Potter books by J.K. Rowling are an excellent example of, not only a success story for the author, but one of a great influence on reading for children and adults.

These books have done so much for children in their desire to learn, all others that come after will want, if not need, to emulate the form of the storyline. As for a child's increasing desire to read, it is because of great writing that children sincerely want to.

As the modern day philosopher, and literary historian, Joseph Campbell, said about *The Hero's Journey,* "There is nothing new under the sun, only just how you make it outshine that sun."

The children of the modern age are not ignorant of reading. They enjoy it. They will continue to read as long as there are great reading choices .

To use one my children's titles as an example of a child appreciating reading, I will use my story entitled *Mom Can I Have a Dragon?* A book I feel I did an excellent job writing, if I do say so myself. It is out of print currently.

I was selling and signing my books at an event when a boy about age eight came up to my table and looked at all the books. He was shy and quiet, and could not bring himself to look up.

His father was right beside him and told him, as many parents do, "Don't touch."

The boy backed off; all the while he kept looking at the books when he focused in on my book about a boy and the dragon he found in his play yard at school.

This boy gently took the book and sat down right there on the floor and began to read to himself. I said to the father that it was alright and that his son just gave me the biggest compliment and reward an author could ever have.

The boy sat right there for the entirety of the book without glancing up or moving at all.

His father said to me, "Wow! I have never seen him read. I did not know he could. I always thought he was just looking at the pictures."

After the boy finished, I asked if he liked the story and he enthusiastically nodded his head yes, not speaking a word. When the father asked him if he would like to have the book, the boy quietly said , "Yes."

The father asked how much it was, thinking it might be expensive. From there I asked to see the book the boy held tightly, and I asked his dad the boy's name.

His name was Jordan, and I signed it-"To my new friend Jordan. Thank You for making my day. T.E.Watson"

I placed it in a bag and told his dad this is a gift from me to Jordan. No charge. The man shook my hand, and Jordan shook my hand, and promptly took the book out of the bag and held it securely to his chest. He walked away wearing the biggest smile I have ever seen on an eight-year-old.

Even though this was a children's book, this is what all writing is about. Enjoyment and reward for the reader.

The rewards are incredible. To write for children or any genre is not always about the money. It is about the times when they find your stories enjoyable and sit down in the middle of a busy floor and read laser focused, then rise with an ear-to-ear grin, not letting go.

I do not know what Jordan was dealing with at home, or at school, or inside himself, but I do know I had something to do with helping this little boy have great success with reading. It may have given the father his first success as well, now knowing his son could read.

That is why we write.

We write because we hope to make someone's life successful, enjoyable, and happier.

## Chapter 3 - Am I Writer Material

When someone has the desire to become a writer, or the ambition to try their hand at becoming an author, they can do no worse than to decide when they have not asked a few questions of themselves.

As I have mentioned before, it is hard, time-taking work. It adopts a long time just to get the time to give yourself writing time. It takes time to give yourself the benefit of the doubt and say you are sticking to a particular time and space to write. Sometimes it is downright impossible. You might have outside activities, homework, children, spouse, responsibilities with your job. Life happens, and it gets in the way. A lot!

The statement may sound a little tongue-in-cheek, but these are items you can consider if you do not know if you are writer material. But ask first: Do you have the time to do any of it?

If you have no time, then why? Just finding out the *Why* question can either make you throw in the towel or if you are stubborn enough, pull your boot straps up and get to writing.

Look at this chapter as a series of things you should consider before the undertaking we as writers love. And after it has become the most important part of our soul, the only thing we could ever do; even after doing things you thought you wanted and went to college to study, it is the only thing we can ever do, or ever will want to do.

It would be the one piece of our lives if someone said we had to stop writing, we would fall into a great funk and have the appearance of a black cloud above us, darkening our existence.

We would tell them to go away; I am writing. Possibly a few other choice things as well.

If you feel in your heart writing is the one career choice for you, then you have a good chance of making a living at it. The successes are few. The significant achievements are even fewer. So if you can answer these questions or you find they resemble any of the previous scenarios, you are most likely a writer.

Writers have a strange reputation of being self-imposed hermits. We are never by ourselves in totality, but we do need to be alone when we are writing.

It is the nature of the work.

If you like to be by yourself in the dark of the night, far from the madding crowds, the ringing of the telephone, the barking of dogs in the alley, the horns blasting from cabs as they speed past the window you use to gain material to write.

Take a breath. Your chances have just increased in your favor.

And as you sit at your desk, lit only by the street light outside your window, you continue to grind away at the writing process while sweat and blood ooze from your forehead, ask yourself: "Why am I doing this?"
You may be surprised.

If, for instance, you find you have writing pads in every room of your house, office, shop, and car, this includes the bathroom, making sure to have new pens or pencils available. Ask yourself, are you nuts? Is this obsessive behavior? Possibly a form of paranoia?

Or are you experiencing a sort of fear in not being prepared if you get a great idea and it needs to be written down, and there is nothing to write it on?

Writers do this all the time. And while you are at it, you buy stock at your favorite big box warehouse store, just to make sure they do not run out of your favorite yellow writing pads and packages of pencils.

How about, when you may be in the middle of a meeting at work? It looks like you're impressing your boss by appearing to write down every topic on the agenda, but in reality, you are risking your job by working on a new story. I am not telling you to do this, but here is a multi-tasking tip… Learn to tap into the conversation as you write. Reporters do this very well.

If you find yourself at a party and you start to look like a person who is really into napkins. Only yours have the writing of new and innovative novels on them. Stuffing your pockets does not always work. Be neat about it at least.

You can get away with this if your friends are understanding. They will say to everyone, "Oh! That's our writer friend. Just keep talking, they won't mind. Just don't ask them for a napkin."

If, when you write something, and someone asks you to read your piece, and you begin to snarl and grow hair on your knuckles, that is time to loosen your collar a bit. Ask them to leave, and then continue with the work.

Crowds and elevators are great areas of gleaning conversational snippets. Be careful, though, in those situations if you start shushing complete strangers around you, so you can hear the dialogue because it may be something that can be used, do the best you can to remember what was said.

At night, when you are in bed, and all tucked in, but you have a computer with you so you can keep working, be as accommodating as your fingers will allow.

If you cannot then go to another room and write. But when your spouse reaches over to ask if you can type more quietly, you may have something to think about there. Relationships can be affected when a writer gets wrapped into a story.

Computers are similar to the writing pads. If you have multiple computers, one in each room of your home for fear you may forget a good idea while walking from the living room to the kitchen, and they are always on. You may want to realize a few things about what writers do.

Sometimes people who are enthusiastic about writing want to be able to write even better than ever, (not always the case here) purchase every piece of writing software known to man because it says it will make your writing better. Don't do it! Run away and hide. But realize this. The only thing that will make your writing better is practice and research on your own. The software will not make your writing better. EVER!

Getting back to the bedroom, Your spouse gets up from what was a good night's rest thinking they heard the alarm clock go off when in reality it is 3 a.m., and it is just you turning on the computer because of what you dreamt would be a great idea and you need to get it down.

Doing this is worse than texting. You are perpetually writing in your head, even when you are driving. You suddenly pull over in heavy traffic and frantically scour for a pad of paper to write it down.

*Remember the yellow pad of paper and pencils and put some in your glove compartment.*

Practice knowing the difference between where to write and where not to write. I would not try to write in traffic. Not really a good idea.

Don't write just because an event that just happened, appears to be great material. If you can't get excited about it, then it isn't worth it.

Thinking about what you write while you are writing, or if you tend to edit your work when writing it, is awkward and non-productive.

*Here's a Tip... Don't do that!*

Finding yourself trying to be dead perfect the first time you set words to paper is senseless. It does not work. *Here's another Tip... Don't do that either.*

It is a waste of time, and it never happens. Live with it. Perfection is an illusion with writing. You can only write about the illusion of perfection.

You will never experience it in your creative process, although it may at some point feel like you have. Never negate that feeling, just don't expect it too often. Strive for excitement in writing instead.

When, at the first moment, you are considering becoming a writer, you know this will take courage and ability to speak in front of crowds, talking with and meeting people, doing interviews, making appearances, and being placed on display.

Knowing you must promote your work because no one else is going to do it as well as you can. And after considering all of it, you are okay with it. You have just taken to biggest step to writer's reality.

If you cannot do this, you will never make it as a writer. Publishing houses, as well as independent authors, must and always will have to promote their work. It is a huge part of the job. There is nothing to fear.

But, if you have a deep anxiety that makes you crawl inside a box when someone approaches you to talk about speaking in public then forget about being a successful writer.

You as a writer should know writing is 10 percent creating, and 90 percent promotion.

From day one, and even before you have been published to the day you die, to be a successful author or writer, you must talk about what you have done.

*"If you done it, it ain't braggin."* *Will Rogers*

Writers, in particular, must get over the upbringing we had when we were told not to bring attention to ourselves. We were told not to be pretentious, or vain or egotistical.

Promotion is NOT any of those.

Promotion is simply the art of being able to converse with those who are interested in what you have to say about what you have achieved in an informative, non-arrogant, and somehow dynamic and exciting fashion. Then hopefully getting them to buy. It does take practice.

If you find you are writing in 3D, then look at these from this point. These are the three sisters. You may be a writer if you find, that no matter what it is, you cannot help yourself but continue to write.

Drive is the first of the three sisters.

If you plant your butt in a spot you can take root and mold your thoughts, a place where all the world around you disappears, and you do that every day for as long as the words come out without hesitation.

Discipline- is the second sister.

Your attitude will be the deciding factor in your success as a writer. If you have the guts to keep at it and never accept the answer *No* on the path you have chosen, then you will achieve the third sister, Desire.

For instance, if you are really a writer, you will know deep inside, that when a dreaded rejection letter comes it is not a personal attack on your existence. It is a business decision. Publishing is a business, not a social club.

Potential writers will get to know the difference between an apple and an orange.

When you get some experience under your writer's belt, and you get to know the submissions processes for publishers, you will be able to tell when the time comes and your project gets accepted for publishing.

Never try to sell your apples to an orange dealer. They will not buy them. By the same token, never try to sell your mystery manuscript to a publisher that deals in how-to books.

Rethink, Re-target, and Re-research. Do it again and with a more refined aim if you don't quite hit the mark the first time. Never take it personally.

Why is this so important?

The publishing industry is thick with writers.
The competition, and there is plenty of competition, is heavy with those who have gone before you and quit. Many have the scars of trying to get their work accepted.

If you know what markets take what, and when they are likely to accept your manuscript, and then if the work has an entirely fresh approach to the topic, then you have a good chance. Remember, this is an industry of being first in line if you can, and being as prepared as possible by being as professional as you can.

You are potentially working with an industry that looks at what will possibly sell the best and the most copies.

What is the first rule after being accepted by a publisher? Start the relationship off right. Be pleasant and friendly. Be grateful. Do what the editors ask of you. If you need re-writes, do them as best and as fast as you can. Don't be sloppy about any of it. They understand the industry far better than you. Don't be a know- it- all.

Publishing houses have kind,considerate , real human beings working for them. They do their very best to find great novels. They especially appreciate writers who can work quickly, accurately, without having to be babysat, and are not demanding.

All real writers usually have a favorite pastime. That activity is finding great enjoyment from reading. If you want to write like the greats, read them without discrimination.

Do you still want to be a writer that gets paid? Most of all, if you have found any volume of courage after all this, your odds have just gone in your favor. Get going. Write down your thoughts and dreams.

Write your book.

# Chapter 4–
# Why Write?

For the many times that I got myself into predicaments and situations which no one should ever get into, my saving grace was the ability to write.

From earning a living in high school and then college, to being an intern at the local paper, having the capacity to write was always a great thing to know. The dumb part was I had kept it all deep inside myself. I was shy and introverted. I wasn't the most popular kid in school, but I was known because of my writing.

My writing opened up many opportunities and helped me get to where I am today. I met prominent writers and others who are still in the publishing industry today. Sports figures, film stars, other well-known, big name authors, international TV personalities, and many others who helped shape my style of writing.

To write well, you must love it. You must want it to be as perfect as you can possibly make it be. You must eat, breathe, and think writing every minute of every day.

Whatever form it takes, it has to come from within your soul, but it should become even more than something you do to fill out a form or do an assignment. In your inner self, you must possess an incredible desire to share with readers your knowledge, opinions, stories, and such.

Being a writer or successful author has its advantages and its drawbacks. Not all the writing you do will be held in high esteem, nor are all the words you write going to be profound, or remembered years after you are gone.

However, if you are fortunate enough to have written anything memorable, you stand a good chance of your name being around for a while.

Much of the time you will have to go through the stale, run-out-of-words, feeling that all writers share. You will think yourself dried up, never to scribe another line. But writers being writers, and the crafters doing that thing they do can also be a temperamental lot. After which they see much of what the ordinary world sees as a depressing story line, or a situation that can change an island into a great ship, or a small mouse who can drive his own car. The simplest of tasks turns into the most difficult chore ever attempted.

But writing is not something you just take out of your pocket and say here you go, read me.

Writers are the beings that take what was once ordinary and, as if by magic, transform that ordinary into the extraordinary. They make the reader feel as if they just experienced the most exciting adventure of their lifetime.

Writing is an adventure, writing is exciting, and writing is the imagination scaling to heights never before reached. There is one thing that writing is most of all. Writing is power!

The writings of an author who writes for the sheer enjoyment of writing is the most dynamic!

With writing, you have the ability to change, mold, and shape minds and emotions into whatever you want. However, you must write well. And to write well takes time and practice. So, get out your pens and pencils, your word processors, your typewriters and computer. Just write!

If you wish to be a writer you must write! Very simple. There is no way around it. That is the only way. Take the time to discipline yourself to write something at least 15 minutes a day. After a while, it will become second nature to you, and it will be something you must do in your everyday routine.

Writing is the power that can build or destroy in a matter of just a few strokes of a pen. It is true; the pen is mightier than the sword. It has been for eons and will be forever.

Now that you have possibly discovered the super powers you possess. Only use these powers for good. There is more than enough bad writing in the world.

Do not allow yourself to be devoured by the lazy writing styles of those who have not made it with their skills, or lack of such skills. It is an easy thing to do, so be careful.

Rather continue the ever-searching quest for the great story. The story that touches every soul and emotion we as humans can stand to bear. The perfect story is the goal. That is what you strive for. Ask this question to yourself. Will I ever be able to write the perfect story?

Perhaps you will. That is what drives us as writers. It will no longer be a question, but a goal.

It will no longer be that writing makes you happy, only that you need to write to be happy!

With the following steps of what writers call the "jazz," you will get an idea that even very successful writers had to pay their dues. Writing is not an easy way to make a living. It takes many hours of processing thoughts and hard work, although it doesn't have to, and it can be the most stress filled way of life you can choose. But the rewards are so great you cannot help but continue writing. It comes out of you like an unexpected sneeze. A storm of words that can either change for the better or discourage.

The great basketball virtuoso Michael Jordan once said, *"Attitude determines altitude."*

He was saying it about the game he loved so much, but when referring to writing it is something to keep in your mind's memory banks and keep there to remember when you start to lose focus with your work and why you are writing. The more positive you are in your thinking, the further up you will go in your achievements.

Your ego can be your worst enemy or your best friend. Many authors, new ones in particular, have a problem when they are discovered or have published for the first time. If you ever find yourself sounding elitist or snobby, where every other word out of your mouth is I, then stand back and listen to yourself speak. Your ego pops up at the worst times and inopportune moments. For instance, during an interview. Your first one always comes to mind.

Remember this. Put your ego in your pocket and keep it there. The ego is a part of the human psyche, so it is not easily put away. It is always with us, whether we want it to be or not. Just be aware when it starts to raise its little head, acknowledge it, and place it back into the cave from which it came.

Authors often have to learn after being smacked about by humility. Being made humble is not an easy bite of crow. It is something you must accept.

It happens at one time or another.

When it happens just take a deep breath and apologize to your inner self and remember what just happened, and then don't do it again. Be conscious
If it occurs again, then it would be time to evaluate your personal attitude as a writer and your work.

Yes, you have worked on it, and only maybe, do you deserve praise for the efforts you placed into it. Do not get ahead of yourself. When that happens, and it will, step back and listen to the words you just spoke and how they sounded. Yes, I have repeated this.

Account for them, and remember if the sentences sounded smooth. Or were they said with an attitude of *I am better than you* snobbery. You will always gain more notoriety with a great attitude, than being an author that appears and sounds arrogant.

It is a far easier method and a finer human quality to remain humble than it is to let your life become angry and hard and thereby allowing your writing to become readable with out question.

# Chapter 5- For the Beginning Beginner

Many times in your life, you will encounter situations when you must decide what is important. There will be times when you find yourself a free run with such a great story that it is the last thing you want to ignore. It will take every beat of your heart and everything else along with it. It will be the blinders that steer your attention from all else, and nothing will be as important as that bit of writing. Your time will be disturbed when life happens. I think you have nothing to worry about is the fact that you were not alone in this disturbance. Great authors also must eat, and pay the electric bill. There were times when I was almost fired or did get fired from jobs for writing when I should have been working.

How dare they insist I stop my writing to work on their job. What your priorities are that you must do the little things that tend to get in your way first. It will always be that way until you become independently wealthy by some means. In the real world, it is sometimes called paying your dues.

As far as family goes, you will always have responsibilities to take care of first. It is just easier to take care of the daily stuff that gets in everyone's way before you dive into your writing. The stress is gone, the phone does not ring, dogs are not barking much, the parents or spouse are watching TV. Little sister is asleep and the world is quieted down enough for you to concentrate on your writing. It is of the most importance that you find some time for you and your writing.

Even if it's just 30 minutes a week or, if things are going well, make it per day. Turn off the video game, turn off the TV, and the stereo, and be sure you have eaten something so your thoughts don't fade. Start by writing whatever comes out of your brain.

Whether it makes sense or not, write it down. Then write letters to friends for 45 minutes. Lastly, continue to write the piece you have painstakingly worked on for days, months or even years. The drive to keep writing is there for you, run alongside and maintain the pace. You will find that if you don't use it, you will lose it.

The discipline to keep up your writing in stressful times of home pressure or job pressure is sometimes difficult to handle.

You know when your heart says you must write and you will write by whatever means it takes.

But do yourself a favor of getting life things done first. Your writing of words will come to you much easier. They will begin to flow like water downstream with all the rocks in life's daily road out of the way.

Remember some simple things.

Get your life stuff done first like chores, homework, family responsibilities, your job; writing comes easier when life gets done for the day.

Ask your parents or your spouse to help with this and let them know that. Let them know you have done everything you were supposed to. At that time, let them know you were going to write and wish not to be disturbed.

Don't get frustrated when you can't get back to your writing. Right words and sentences are patient. They will be there waiting for you to return.

Detach yourself from the ruckus that will disturb your thought processes.

Find a special quiet place for you to write.

And last and certainly not least, write about everything. You tend to get better at it when you do.

# Chapter 6- They

*A little tongue-in-cheek commentary*

Throughout time there has always been a group of curious authorities only known to everyone as *they*. *They* have no name to speak of, only an association to which *they* are referred. Evidently, they do many things and have many opinions, and more often than we prefer to acknowledge, have an affinity along with a unique talent to know and say everything in an educated and knowledgeable fashion.

We do not have any idea where *they* come from, nor do *they* for that matter. But for some stupid reason, we follow what *they* say with religious ferocity.

So why are *they* so important? We never know who *they* are, we do not know the importance of this odd group of authoritarians. For some reason, we have put them on a pedestal, and there *they* have stayed.

Did *they* go to a unique teaching facility of higher learning thereby making them omnipotent?

This, *they*, everyone speaks of so highly must be those who would like to have everyone think are as important as *they* think they are. But there is no way to cement down an absolute fact that they are what *they* say they are. *They* have no proof that they are even real. But they always show up when there is information to be had, or something snotty to be told.

*They* always seem to be there whether or not *they* are needed. *They* run in the highest circles and know the most celebrity of celebrities because someone said *they* should.

So, who are *they*, we ask?

I will tell you.

When it comes to writing, and beginning writers, in particular, this *they* is the one being who has ruined more careers than any other reviewer, editor, or publisher.

Even the writers themselves don't have any idea who the *theys* in the world are, only because the writer has not had any run-ins with them. It may take some time, but they will appear when *they* feel like showing up at an event or scene.

*They* are rude, impetuous, rumor filled, gossip mongers, who have nothing to say cordial about anything, or anyone. Then, there are those around them, listen to what *they* say are made into authorities by someone who said, *they, should be.* But does this matter? No, not at all.

*They* are the only ones who think they matter. It is when *they* begin to get in the way of someone's goal or path do *they* cause trouble and doubt.

If you remember, the new writer often falls flat after having listened to the comments *they* have made. Usually, *they* are the cause of great strife, and it is because *they* have no business being where *they* are, to begin with.

It is because of their opinions that *they* bring fear and a downtrodden thought to appear in the minds of new writers. The new writer is then put in an awkward place. Do they pay attention to what *they* have said or do they ignore them and go on if *they* get in the way?

*They* have this related method of ruining lives and goals. *They* take what may have started out as a wonderful idea and because *they* have said something about it, make it disappear.
Then *they* always have something negative to say.

"Oh, it was not supposed to be anyway." Or, "It was never going to get off the ground." And because *they* said it, makes it the truth.

Discouragement is the writers worst enemy and at all cost need to be avoided. But discouragement becomes the nourishment for what *they* say.

I say nonsense!

*They* only get in the way, and *they* are the one most single cause of failure. By not paying any attention or giving any value to what *they* have to say, your writing will come to life without fear of what *they* have to say.

# Chapter 7–
# Quitting Your Day Job

Being a full-time author and balancing the role is hard in today's economy. Historically, many well-known authors have carried alternative ways of making a living, because royalties from contracts from their publishers arriving on time was rare.

They all had this one commonality; they had to eat, pay bills, and take care of family.

Times were tough, and cash money was in short supply. Not many books sold other than in the larger cities such as New York City or Philadelphia.

The Midwest was developing, and towns and cities were popping up all over, and regional economies were growing, but not substantially.

Authors often sold copies of stories by subscription in newspapers or magazines. The printing industry was a slow and cumbersome enterprise, and distribution of any news or articles sometimes took weeks to arrive at a town. Some towns had their own newspapers, and if they were fortunate enough to have a known writer live in the same town or area, they would be asked to write for the paper as well. Writers weren't paid much, but it was something.

During the early 1900s distribution of newspapers and magazines began to shift gears and it became quicker to reach a store or newsstand, but not by much.

In the era of authors of the early 1800s there was virtually no economy except that which was done by trading, or exchanging services, or was paid for with money if you had it.

There was no shame in this. Keeping care of yourself and your family was honorable and necessary. No one was going to cause any grief and say you were not successful because you had to take a job.

Being an author was something that meant being put on a pedestal and appreciated. If you fell from grace as a writer and needed to take on extra work, there must be something wrong with you or your work.
Not so.

It was not until the 1900s feelings about working extra, no matter who you were or what you could do, that attitudes changed. No longer were you thought of as a failure. The large publishers were struggling to stay in business, and authors were still going the route of publishing their works themselves. It was not easy due to the high cost of production.

It is still an expensive venture, especially if you are planning to publish and bind in hardcover.

It is possible to use authors, and their writings as a barometer of sorts, to gauge the sociological topics of that time and that included the economy. Not by the economy itself, but by the rate of job positions being taken and held by authors and writers.

Here are a few...

Kurt Vonnegut- *Slaughterhouse-Five, Breakfast of Champions.* He was the first to open a Subaru car dealership in 1957. He was not very good at selling the cars, so it gave him time to write while waiting for someone to show interest in the cars.

Jack London – *Call of the Wild, White Fang* among many others.
Jack London was an oyster pirate. Meaning he stole fish from the traps and nets of other fishermen. He was also an unsuccessful gold miner.

Charles Dickens- *A Christmas Carol, Oliver Twist,* and many others- Mr. Dickens worked in a shoe polish factory from the age of 12. During this time of brutal child labor situations he was able to craft the characters for *Hard Times and Oliver Twist.*

Agatha Christie- So many mysteries I cannot name them. Agatha worked as an apothecary's assistant. She used her pharmacology experience to reference the information she used in her story lines.

John Steinbeck- *The Grapes of Wrath, Of Mice and Men, Tortilla Flat, Travels with Charlie.* and many more.
John Steinbeck was a construction worker, a war correspondent in WWII and held jobs in Salinas, Los Gatos, and San Francisco, California.

George Orwell - *1984*
George held the distinct position of an East Indian Imperial Police Officer.

Fodor Dostoevsky - *Crime and Punishment, The Brothers Karamozov.*
Engineer for the Russian military.

Arthur Conan Doyle – *Sherlock Holmes*
Conan Doyle was a surgeon in private practice, where he drew much of his conversational elements between Holmes and Dr. Watson from his experiences.

Now there are those crazy moments when your writing comes to you as a craving so intense you must put that idea to paper straight away or lose it forever.
It is those times that if you don't immediately scribble

words on something, you may lose altogether, your ability to create. These times come and go on a daily basis, and it is hardly likely your words will ever come back.

I'm here to tell you that the single most important aspect of your daily work is to concentrate on the way you make a living. When you work at your J-O-B job, don't allow your writing craving to overwhelm your bread-winning.

Stephen King, John Steinbeck, Michael Crichton, and many others had regular jobs. The numbingly mundane kind that brought in some money when weeks, and sometimes months and years, produced not one single literary item suitable for submission, or royalties did not arrive.

If you were thinking of quitting your day job, go outside, kick your shoes off and run around in freezing weather. You need to wake up! No writer ever, unless they are suddenly independently wealthy, quit their job.
It should never happen. Don't do it.

Do you have a job outside your writing career? It is not a shameful thing. You are among the most famous writers who had families, and who needed to make sure there was bread on the table and clothes on their backs.

Seldom do writers, particularly children's writers, have the luxury of writing for a living. I've held many jobs since I came of age. The first was as a paperboy, the most exotic as an assistant at a rehab center for and preserve for big

cats, like lions and tigers. No, there were no bears.
Some more regular jobs were a paint salesperson at a
hardware store, and of course, everyone has done fast food.
Bottom line, writing pays little when you are starting
out, so, it is fine to have a job to supplement your income.
When work is over at the end of the day you go home,
play with your kids, and talk to your husband or wife. It
may appear easy, but it is an ultra-important part of the
writing life.

If you must write, find a schedule for yourself. John
Steinbeck had a routine. He would get up early in the
morning and write letters about what he needed to do for
characters in books he was writing, even if he had written
about them the previous day, to get the juices flowing. For
a short time, he would just write down whatever came
into his head, then he would go to work on his actual
project or assignment and go for about two hours. At
one point in his career, then he would trundle off to work
at a warehouse job in San Francisco. With his job day
complete, he would come home and be with his family.

Every day he did this and unless he was on assignment
for some publisher. He did it like clockwork. His family
appreciated his efforts to be with them.

So, take care: your priorities are, until you are making
a regular check from your ongoing writing assignments,
family, family, and family, in that order.
You go through the frustration, impatience, and aggravation
of dying to grab that fantastic idea or not getting it

right then and there. Just remember your responsibility. Although that frustration will stay with you for some time and you wish you had not had a job. Take the time to breathe and remember why you are working.

Yes, there may come a time when you feel so good and that you must write at all costs. Well, take that drive and sit on it. Don't say, "take this job and...," you know the rest. Control yourself. Write down your idea, so you don't forget it. Just bear in mind, the writing career you have chosen is a slow row to hoe. Don't be impatient with your work or yourself.

Take that all so important deep breath. Keep writing when you can, and success will happen. Rome was not built in a day. Neither is anyone's writing career.

The best writers have never been overnight successes. Being slow is the nature of the publishing industry. Just bear in mind that everything happens with good timing.

# Chapter 8-
# Success in the Beginning

All writers are curious. Especially the new ones. They always want to know everything about writing. That is an impossibility. Unless, of course, you have an unlimited amount of years and will never age. However, learning how to write is one thing, the actual writing is another, and getting it published is entirely different altogether.

Having been asked the question so many times, "How do I become a writer?" I decided to answer it differently. I put a question back to the would-be writer and say, "Do you mean, "How do you get published?"

Then, the a-ha moment happens. The would-be writer's eyes brighten, and the reply is usually, "Yes, that's it! How do I get published?"

The answer to this one is not a short one. It can take as long as years to answer it. The only real answer to the question is this. Experience and time are your best teachers, and it is a long class.

There is no short way to teach this. The silly question new writers ask of those more experienced is, "Could I call you or email you and pick your brain?"

It is impossible to show anyone what the publishing industry is like over the phone or by email. As any experienced author will tell you, talking to someone over a phone or writing an email will take a considerable amount of time.

Consulting is not what we do. We are writers, and we write to make money. If you want to make money too, you will grab that thought and keep it close to your soul. We do not do this to make ourselves feel good. The concept of writing is to share and possibly help humankind with what we have to say. However, you asked how do I become a writer?

The real answer is, "Without anyone's help."
You are on your own in most cases.

It is not that experienced authors do not like new writers. It is because the time it takes is long and none of you can afford to pay us any reasonable sum for our labor and knowledge. For the most part, none of you consider paying an experienced writer at all for their help. You have taken time away from their livelihood and cost them money. But you are thinking, "They don't need the money they are successful writers."

Some of us receive a regular royalty payment, every three to four months depending on our contract with our publisher, but in between time, bills still need to be paid. Taking valuable time away from an author is like taking food from their family's mouths.

Most of us are patient and kind people who will help in hopes you will not want the universe in one answer. And you might actually offer to pay something. You can take the chance of asking an author for help, but you may get turned down.

When I am sitting at my desk working on an article or book, I do not tolerate being disturbed by anyone. I usually let out a disgusted sigh, and my right eyebrow raises. A moment like that is one which will foul up a day or a writing rhythm so fast; it is best not to be anywhere around when it happens. That is why writers have their spaces to create their worlds. It allows them to focus on their work.

But, if you need to talk to someone about getting started with your writing, make an appointment and then be sure to keep the appointment. NO EXCUSES within three minutes of the time. If you are late, you won't get another chance to ask your questions. You are, after all, asking an enormous favor of someone who has climbed the ropes, gotten the blisters of experience, and knows what it takes to get published in the real world. All writers must go through this path to find what is the way for their journey. They cannot take the trail of someone else. It does not work.

You can study and read and practice, but you must find your method and voice to become the writer you are to be. No one will hold your hand or talk you through the process every minute of every day. There is not enough time in the day to do that.

There is a path you can take. It is the appropriate way for a new writer. It is a long trail. The writing pioneers explored this method long before you made the decision to become a writer. Master Authors, those who have come up through the ranks and paid their dues, have written their experiences, techniques, practices and opinions into published books knowing you would want to find the information and become a writer.

Go to your bookstore or online bookstore. Find these references and read them. It will allow you to research on your own time and you won't feel as though you are taking someone's valuable time. It will probably be cheaper as well.

Use your local library and ask to see the reference section on writing and publishing. If you have internet access, use it to death. There is a massive amount of information about getting started in writing and how to be published in whatever format you want. Study it all first and then decide, not before. Don't go into it with the big dream of becoming famous.

One step at a time is what it takes.
You start with baby steps, then learn to walk and then run.
If that is the journey you are to take, it will work for you.

Be careful, be patient, and be humble on the journey.
Follow those three throughout your quest, and you will
succeed.

# Chapter 9- Talent

In writing, there is no natural talent. There is just exceptional ability and knowledge of the English language or whatever language you happen to be speaking or writing. There is also unique, imaginative ability that goes along with good storytelling and construction. There is someone who has been dedicated in their practice of writing.

Let's say you have some ability. Let's also say only the people with it ever get far enough to suspect they don't.

I know that sounds strange, but it is entirely accurate. Vincent van Gogh was one of the most unconfident artists of his time, and yet his works are only now selling for millions.

Unfortunately, he is no longer with us. I hope you don't have to get to that point for your creative work to sell.

You can probably think of others who fit the mold. The anxiety of writing gets into the guts of all writers. It is incredible. It does not matter if they are professional writers or first timers. That nail-biting, waking up in the middle of the night wondering feeling, did I double space the manuscript I just submitted? These stomach growlings affect them all.

The more professional a work appears, the unwanted emotions will effectively turn against themselves. Because the more it makes you wonder if things are just right, the more you will pay attention to the details you need to check and double check before placing that effort of blood, sweat, and ink into the mail slot.

Now, to the scary part.

It has been said by many, "People who can write should write."

That is not always the case. It is true however that just because you can write doesn't always mean you should make a career out of it. You may be happy doing something else for a living. There is no dishonor in that. It takes many years of training, practice, and classes to get a feel for the English language and the mechanics of the language you are using.

Punctuation, spelling and all the rest, go right along with the entire writing process. This is something you should have learned in school.

But then, you start to think, what is my story about and how am I going to write about it?
Now it begins to become involved.

Do you know about the hook and plot, subplots, character development and much more knowledge than you may have at this time?

Do you know the jargon of the industry? It does help if you do. Being aware of the worlds you are creating is a plus. If you have no idea what you are doing, then why are you doing it? Have you thought about the reasons you want to do this and why?

If not, start. Determining why you want to be a writer is not an easy decision. It takes time and some logic to figure it out. Many sacrifices get made whether you like it or not, or you expect it or not. It will show its head in the most unlikely of places and times.

If you have some talent, and that may be for whatever reason you think you do (not a bad thing), start by taking the small baby steps we spoke of earlier. Learn everything you can about the genre you wish to emulate.

Learn from reading the great writers of your genre, including writers and authors of the 1700s, 1800s, and 1900s. Absorb as much as you possibly can. Study everything.

Without those writers, we would not be where we are today. Research them in ways you never thought you were able to before. Ask questions of yourself.
Read and dissect each and every sentence, every paragraph, every punctuation mark and ask yourself these questions.

Why did they write it that way? Why did they use that word instead of that one, etc.? How come they used that punctuation mark? If I did this story in another fashion and wrote it this way, or that, how would it read? "What if," the story to an extreme.

Examine it under a writing microscope.
Take your time, and it will work in your favor.

# Chapter 10- Commitment

When the days and weeks go by so fast, and so many issues happen during it all, your goals for the week transform into a useless pile. Nothing gets done. When that happens, your personal frustration elevates, and you need to re-focus and get back into the writing groove. Even though you may have done some editing, rewriting of projects in process, and maybe even got emails cleaned up, you may still consider the time wasted, that valuable time that you cannot get back.

It is all well and good, but it does not advance your progress. Yes, it does sound selfish. Sometimes in the world of writing, you must keep your creative juices flowing. You may as well eat bonbons and sit in front of the television if you are going to waste time.

But ask yourself this, would you want to do that, or would you want to get writing again and get on it.

Personally, and in my opinion, if I started to feel I needed an excuse to write it would not be worth the effort.

Finding an excuse might send a signal you have begun to give up. That is not necessarily true. My personal methods of keeping in the groove are vast and varied, but this feeling of lazy or not feeling like you want to write, happens to us all. It is not a good feeling. It is a dangerous emotion that can be overwhelming to writers. They begin to think they have failed and no longer can be the writer they have worked so hard to become.

We are such an emotional lot, and can be temperamental at times; we can ill afford to fall into this melancholy. It takes us over and holds us hostage for who knows how long. We have no choice but to keep creating, no matter how unproductive a week you have had.

This writer's depression of sorts can easily drag you away from the writing you have spent so much time. The hours and days, the thought processes, the building of the piece from the beginning are all valuable and must not be considered a waste of your time.

If writers set out to write the Great American Novel, and after finishing, found it to be garbage, all they need to do is consider it another version or draft that needs a bit of help and keep on working on it.

The work will tell you when it is ready. It will tell you loudly and clearly, and you will be confident with what you have accomplished.

It is called commitment, and before any writer can start, experienced or new, it is the first thing to consider before setting out on this journey.

The act of writing is like preparing your products in a farmer's market. Let's say you're not exactly sure you have a marketable product. The product needs to look its best for it to sell or even catch buyers. That is why we cannot allow the feeling of worthlessness to overcome us. You have to be willing to work hard and go out into the cold, damp world every day to catch the early morning buyers, the publishers, and the agents and editors. Commitment in writing is never giving up despite the rejection notices, despite the criticisms, despite seeing everyone else's book or article getting published. (when you feel your work should have been put in print a long time ago).

Commitment also means having the gut feeling that you will soon be a published author.

If you were in a canoe and paddling through rough water, you would not jump out of the canoe, right? You stay in the canoe, and you ride out the fast and scary whitewater. Writing is the same. Ride out the rough water. It does get better and easier.

Sometimes the rough water does get to you, and you need to find a shallow spot off the rapids somewhere to take a break in calmer waters. That's perfectly fine. We all need to do that. When it does occur, make sure you're ready to get back into the water. That's the hard part. When we realize that no matter how we get there, we still must get there, it is essential we are emotionally prepared for the journey. And when we do get there we will have such satisfaction and gratification we will not mind getting back into that rough water again to start a new adventure. By that time you know where the potentially difficult rocks and deeper water are.

You will know what to do when you run into them.

Giving up just because you are not getting the results you hoped for when you wrote the work. The fact is, it is sometimes that way. The reasons can be anything if it doesn't read like you thought it should. Leave your pity party and get back to work.

Yes, the frustration will be there, but once you are back in the saddle again and your horse is traveling at a good gallop, you will get to the destination and in good shape.

Commitment is a process. Not only must you believe in what you are doing, but you must also, with all your soul, believe in your work and you. If you cannot do that, stop what you are doing. Turn off the computer or put your pencil down and quit.

Writers can't afford to do this if they feel their work is worth the grief and time.

In two of my children's stories *A Place to Be* and *Henry The Little Kite*, the main characters throughout the stories, know that to achieve a goal they must never give up.

Never Give Up!

## Chapter 11- Drive

Keep going! Go over, under, around and through. Don't let anything stop you from getting or achieving your goal. Use every opportunity to conjure, percolate, and just plain think about, that story in your head. Get it on the piece of paper. Keep a pad with you. Do whatever you need to do, but work on your goal all the time.

All writers do this. If they don't have the time to do it, they find a time to do it.

You are in total control here. You are the only one who can do this massive task. It will be daunting. The people around you who do not understand will tell you to quit what you are doing and go back to a real job.

I say, Ha!

You don't see them having the ambition or the dream to write a story. You don't see the naysayers with any drive to create, and possibly hold a book of their own as a result. These people are the ones who hold doors shut for those who need to go through. These are the people who do not want you to succeed. They do not want to be left behind by themselves.

They had their chance. Maybe they failed or quit for one reason or another. Whatever the case, it is not your fault they did not make it. *Fear got to them.*

Being afraid kills many creative endeavors. The only way to keep from falling into this trap is to learn how to ignore the fear. It is not easy, but it isn't hard either. It all rests on your opinion of your work and your personal philosophy. Try meditating for a few minutes before you start writing each day. Remember to breathe and stretch throughout your writing time. Smile as you write. It works.

Most of all, laugh at the ones who say you're not any good; you don't stand a chance. There are better writers than you in the world. So what? Even they had to start somewhere, and they were not aways as good as they are now.

Deflect the word no, and the negative attitudes people project in your direction.

You have nothing to fear.

# Chapter 12-

# The Importance of Name

Having just gone through some pieces I wanted to include in a new collection of writings and essays, I realized I did not include my name on a few. I don't know why I would have forgotten to do that, but I did.

Having done so brought a quote to mind by Mark Twain, "If you are not happy with your work don't put your name on it." I found this odd that I would even consider not placing my author's pseudonym on any of my writing.

I realized I might have been tired, in a hurry, or just careless. But the point is, I always placed my name on my work. I write daily, and I needed to identify what it is I have written and when I wrote it. The purpose for this is to keep track of my personal writing.

The essays I composed years ago and those I have written recently are important and as the years go by it is easy to forget when I wrote them. However, forgetting is not a good excuse anymore.

Placing your name on your work is important. So much so, it is the first form of protection from plagiarism and overall theft by others who may have thought they wrote the article, or in some cases like your work so much they just figure it's okay to take it as their own. That is why we have copyright laws. They are there to protect intellectual property from theft.

Your name is the most important item you must remember to put on your work. Name is the single most important identifier on anything you do. You need to put your name on everything you write, whether or not you are happy with what you've written. I recommend identifying yourself with your actual name, and then with your pseudonym, if you have one. Also, do not neglect the date and time. It nails down ownership and seals the deal in making your work yours.

Look up the copyright laws, or contact a copyright/ intellectual rights attorney for more clarity on how to copyright. I do not recommend trying to do a copyright without an initial consultation. If you are unsure about any of this process, take the time and a few dollars and get the consult. It will help you feel better about protecting your work and how it is protected.

The copyright form, TX 40, is quickly filled out and understood; anything else should be left to the intellectual property attorneys to do the heavy lifting. There are a limited number of these attorneys in the United States, so they are always busy. Be patient if you cannot get an appointment right away.

The more your name appears on your works, no matter what work it is, the more your name will be recognized. The more recognition, the more sales, and notoriety you will receive.

Your name is a good thing to put on your writing.
Use it wisely and protect it.

# Chapter 13- A Mixed Bag

You have all heard the saying that writing for children is the most difficult way to get published. It is a very accurate statement for a reason, but it is not a reason that has to keep you down and at bay. No matter what type of writing you are doing it is hard work. This is a general fact. It takes an extreme amount of time and can often eat up months and even years of creative time.

Many writers in this industry have acquired an attitude which dictates having an elitist state of mind. These types frankly, drive me crazy, but they do have their place. They are here to make us all much more driven to succeed. However, it does not mean you need to develop a bad attitude, especially one pointed at a potential colleague. I learned this early in my career. These are the character types that make you wonder if they started out by hanging out in coffee shops with little or no lighting, filled with rancid, severely menthol filtered, cigarette smoke.

They could be seen sitting in the back of a coffee house wearing a cheap tweed jacket with patches on the elbows, topped off with a black faux beret from the Left Bank of the Seine in Paris or the local thrift store. Oh, and I must not forget the horn-rimmed sunglasses.

The stereotype did exist many years ago. The attitude was one of artistic snobbery and rebellion towards society. A better than any other artist, nose in the air, type of thinking. A holier than thou persona that left many writers with a sour taste, so much so, it might make you wonder if attempting to write what you hope would be a book someday, would be worth doing at all.

This image is the artistic fifties of the writer slash author who has nothing better to do than wait for the inspiration of the political atmosphere to feed them whatever may come in the form of verbal protein.

It left a visual negative in your mind which made you wonder what the hard, black coffee drinking, cig smoking, writer was writing, or if any of it was worth reading at all.

These so-called avant-garde writers make us all nuts! They make editors especially crazy.
These are the ones who are nonchalant, with the exaggerated hand gestures and all. The I cannot write until the artistic energy comes to them, types.
La de freak – in da! Get over yourselves!

There is a definite difference between the two types of people who write.

There are those who write just for writing's sake. The writing has no structure or plan. It is simple, yet, decent, good writing.

Real writers are those who spend time going after ideas. They go after ideas. They search them out with a club, as Jack London wrote. Searching and then finding what may be, for them, the great story, or at least one that appears to be the great story.

They keep going after the next one after that and never quit searching. Time after time, it is a never-ending quest. They are the writers who write the excellent work people need to be reading. There are many fantastic writers. They don't know it because they are emotionally and creatively held down.

The ones who are doing the holding are fearful, and possibly the most ego-filled persons in the industry. But the fact that they are fearful is what makes them the easiest to ignore.

"If you are trying to write a book, forget it, you'll never make it." they say. These are the *better than everyone*, types that need to quiet down a bit. If only because they are a pain in the ear and need to be told to shut the hell up.

Take your writing and find out what the rules are as best you can. Then be daring enough to break the so-called sacred rules of publishing and grammar and punctuation. Any professional author will tell you there are no real rules to writing. Just learn everything as best you can and practice. Please note- I am not saying to ignore grammatical instances. There is never enough proper grammar. However, take a look at The Elements of Style by Strunk and White. It has been a writer's best friend for a long time.

This short volume is a vital member of my personal library and has helped me through so many issues. I have it right on my desk. In my opinion, it should be in every writer's library. *The Elements of Style* is not a large reference book, but one that you should use as you are writing, and kept right on your desk.

There are hundreds of reference magazines and books by writers, for writers about writing, techniques, methods, opinions.

Go to your local bookstore and check the books out. Find the books that apply to your needs and genre.
Take your time and briefly, study them in the store.
If you find them to be helpful, buy them.

(The bookstore is not a library. Don't read the entire book in the store like many people do. It's rude and inconsiderate, not only to the business owners, but also to the authors who wrote the book. You have taken away their livelihood by not purchasing their work.) Where were we? Oh yes. Back to finding a book to study.

Just, temporarily mind you, shrug off the constant rules of the book ogres who tell you there is only one way and if you do not do it that one way you will never succeed.

The children's book publishing industry was started by one company back in the early 1900s, and it was an afterthought for their business. It was never supposed to happen.

The concept of children's books, at the time, was a way to pacify children, not enhance their minds. A literary babysitter was all books were.

The industry is such now that if it does not change for the better and ignore the prolific psychological interference so intrusive in most of the modern or contemporary juvenile books, and get back to the ways of good old-fashioned storytelling, it will succumb to the world of computer games and television.

Remember this-
Only those who have the real talent, ever get far enough to doubt having any talent at all. Creative minds are a worrisome lot. They are always wondering if someone will like their work and for a good reason. Remember this as well. The publishing industry and becoming published is a crapshoot.

Keep going. Ignore the ignorant who maliciously criticize. There will be plenty, no doubt.

These are those who project such negativity, you, as a writer, can ill afford to give any attention. Only be critiqued by those who you know are legitimate critics and have been for some time (a long time preferably), have the experience, and have books or articles with which you are familiar. Just don't do it. You will regret it.

Fair warning; I am harsh in these next paragraphs.

I write this way on purpose. These are the critics who claim so much and know so little. It is similar in a way to a doctor calling themselves a plumber, and yet, they know nothing about pipes. It goes for anyone who shoots out claims of knowledge and has none. You know what I mean.

There are those out there who only talk about writing, and never do any of their own. These are the dangerous ones. They claim to know all there is about the craft and have no experience whatsoever in being published. You cannot depend on the opinion of anyone who has never been published or has less than two books in print.

Save yourself the heartache, but expect the truth, and don't expect them to be pleasant all the time. Any professional reviewer will tell you the sometimes hard truth. It is up to you to be professional or to at least act like one if you can. It is your choice.

A critique is not a personal jab at your writing or your writing abilities. It is what you have asked the critic or reviewer to do. If you ever ask to be critiqued, do not be surprised when the reviewer looks at your work in an unfavorable light.

Not everyone will like everything all the time. If you are not professional enough to carry the load of a critique, good or bad, then you are not ready to be a writer.

Ask yourself some questions to re-evaluate your motives and find the honest answers within yourself to become real with your reasoning of wanting to become a published author.

If you have found you have more negative responses than positive, you should then possiblt reconsider the idea of and do something else other than writing for publication.

Not everyone is suited for this carreer. There is not shame or dishonor in the thought. Not everyone is a plumber, or a teacher either.

Re-evaluate why you might have wanted to try your hand at becoming an author. but if you come up with more excuses than reasons to keep going, then you can easily determine that you may not be destined for the writer's journey.

# Chapter 14-
# Setting the Scene

In a book entitled *My Favorite Story* published by the International Magazine Company Inc. of New York, New York, and printed in March 1929, was one particular story that commands the attention it deserves. *Humoresque* by Fanny Hearst is a story written for that era, and it is about one family in the Jewish ghetto of Hell's Kitchen in New York City.

It starts like this, and it's the perfect description of a district in an area of New York City. It is the introduction, the scene setting, that will give you the full visual presence and description of an area so vast and yet so different.

It begins like this-

*"On either side of the Bowery, which cuts through like a drain to catch its sewage, everyman's land, a wreaking march of humanity and humidity, steams with the excrement of seventeen languages, flung in Patois of*

*life from tenant windows, fire escapes, curbs, stoops, and cellars whose walls are terrible and spongy with fungi. By that impregnable chemistry of race, whereby the red blood of the Mongolian and the red blood of the Caucasian become as if oil and water in the mingling. Mulberry Street, bounded by 16 languages, runs it's intact Latin length of push carts, clotheslines, naked babies, drying vermicelli; black-eyed women in rhinestone combs and perennially big with child; whole families of buttonhole makers who first saw the blue and gold light of Sorrento, bent at homework around a single gas flare; pomaded barbers of 1000 Neapolitan armors. And then, just as suddenly, almost without osmosis and by the mirror stepping down from the curb, Mulberry becomes Mott Street, hung in grillwork balconies, the moldy smell of poverty touched up with incense. Oriental whose feet shuffle and whose faces are carved out of Satinwood. Forbidden women, their white drugged faces behind upper windows. Yellow children, incongruous enough in western clothing. A draughty area away within the bleak of gaslight in a black well of a descending staircase. Show windows of Jade and tea in Chinese porcelains. More streets emanating out from Mott like a handful of crooked rheumatic fingers, then suddenly the Bowery again, cowering beneath Elevated trains, where men burn down to the butt end of soiled lives passed in and out and out and in the knee-high swinging doors, a veiny- nosed, acid eaten race in themselves."*

Now bear in mind that in 1929 and the 20s overall, we called humankind by different words so there's no need for fear of being politically correct or anything that would be considered offensive. Political correctness had no bearing in that era. It is what the writer witnessed. Simply because that's the way people were, and people excepted it. It has no bearing on today's society either if you are truthful in your writing.

The reason I put this in this particular chapter was this; it was because this is one of the perfect ways and perfect scene introductions that any one author or writer could have ever written. It describes the people, it describes the area, it describes everything they were in and experiencing. This method has long been used by writers and has developed and evolved into a process filmmakers use as well.

The writer, the author, starts out as if they have a wide angle lens, it examines the entire area, and then it becomes smaller in size, more personal, and more intimate. It starts that way because the best way to begin any story is to give the reader a feeling of where they are.

It gives the reader a more personal knowing of the characters in the story. It also gives the audience a chance to use all of their senses, hearing, sight, smell, touch, and emotion. All necessary to the reader.

They need to use them all on their journey while reading what the author has put to paper.

It is the author's job to help the reader feel. It is the author's duty to assist the reader on their journey into the words that the author has imagined, has developed, or has conceived and built. And it is the author's job to be sure that the reader comes away with the same feeling that the author experienced when they wrote it.

It is vital that the author can construct a clear and meaningful sentence each and every time. If it takes forever to form a sentence that makes sense, then it does. There is no schedule for writing. If they cannot, they need to practice. And if they cannot practice why did they become a writer?

*Remember this-Good writing takes time. Great writing is personal opinion.*

*T.E. Watson*

If the reader finds a book or article they want to read, and they get excited about the piece while reading it, they get tied into it; they become part of the author's world.

However, if the reader becomes disappointed in the story, the author has failed in their duty to write something that any reader would want to read time and time again.

Not everything is going to be crystal clear, as far as the author is sometimes concerned. What they get excited about is entirely different from what the reader will.

Not everything succeeds. There have been many times when what we would like to write does not meet our expectations, and so it falls to the dirt suffering from literary starvation and lack. The writing is weak and dies. Nothing can help it.

For the writer, this is not their worst nightmare. If their words cannot reach the minds of the readers they're targeting, then there is no reason for them to be writers. If, once in a while, things happen to make the words unclear, for instance, if they're sick or they are having trouble concentrating or are experiencing some difficulty in their writing, the creativity that many writers can have problems with is just not there.

It occurs more often than not. Every creative person goes through this. Annoying as it may be, it is something most creative people deal with on a regular basis.

The trouble we as writers tolerate is the gremlin called writer's block. Personally, I do not believe it exists.
In my opinion, this becomes an excuse for lazy writing to set in, thereby, and seemingly causing, the so-called writer to stop. It is an excuse and not a good one.

There is always something to write. Don't sweat this.
Keep this in mind if you have decided to become a writer. So write without fear of criticism. Write as if you have nothing in your way.

No one will ever give you permission except yourself.

# Chapter 15-

# A Philosophy of Writing

There are various beliefs regarding written form. How to write, what to write, etc. Many writers believe their writing is the end all to end all. They write the Great American Novel, and it will bring in so much of the almighty dollar, no matter who reads it, it will prove they are the best of the best.

That is all well and good if you prefer to have that mindset.

As for me,in my opinion, there is a far better way to project your work and your beliefs in what writing truly is.

I was invited to attend and be part of a panel discussion on the topic of children's book writing and our feelings on the publishing industry of that time.
All the members got the same questions. One question, in particular, was, "What would you do as an author if a publisher gave a considerable

advance of one million dollars? Would you let them do anything they wanted with your manuscript or not?" We all answered in the same fashion, except for one in particular arrogant author.

This author said straight out; "You, (targeting me) must be nuts to say I would not take that amount of money."

As far as he was concerned, the publisher could have his work and do whatever they wanted with it.

I had the opportunity to answer beforehand that my writing was not about the monetary return. If a publisher were to take what I wrote and completely change its voice and meaning, after handing me a huge amount of money, I would not accept it.

I would tell them "Thanks but no thanks."

My personal beliefs and my ethical practices were not going to change because of a wad of money.
I refused to become a sellout. My personal philosophy is one of which my writing must be kid friendly and one that a child would want to read time and time again.
I do not believe any writer needs to become a sellout for any amount of money or any reason. That is not what writing is.

My belief in my work and the words I place to paper is reliable, and healthy. It is as strong as the writing can be, at least for the time being.

If, at some point, I feel the work needs to go through a revision or twelve, or re-writing in general as it often does, so much the better.

As writers, we must take ourselves out of ourselves, and the rest is easy. By no means do I want to express this is an easy task. It is not.

Our egos are our worst enemy. It gets in the way. It causes us grief, anxiety, worry. It often makes us seem arrogant or foolish. It can ruin, what would have been, great publishing deals. Our inner selves need to step out of the way and let the infinite powers do their thing and help make the writing easier. Not perfect, just more comfortable.

When the ease of writing happens, it works, it flows, and it makes sense. It should never be a struggle. If it is, you are paddling upstream against the flow, and nothing works.

The late great songwriter and musician John Lennon wrote in one of his lyrics, "relax your mind and float downstream."

This line is as valid as any can be. When you are physically relaxed and have a relaxed state of mind, in anything you do, the creativity or task arrives with the smooth glass-like surface of a lake on a calm day. It will, enter quietly and with purpose, and with such constant flow it will become alive for you and your reader.

Do not be concerned with the financial aspect of writing or selling your work, at least not yet.

Do not be concerned with the success of writing. Do not worry if anyone will like your stuff after being read. If you put all that aside and can relax during your process, writing will become an event.

It will bring all your hopes to the forefront, and they will arrive on their own, in their own time, and when they are supposed to, naturally.

The groove, as some writers call it, is that perfect wave, that smooth downhill when skiing. It is an essential personal place where everything becomes peaceful. That place is what transforms you into a writer.

Now you are saying, "I am a writer. I write and think and bring thoughts and ideas together. Doesn't that mean I am a writer?"
Nope, it does not. That only means you know how to write words and know some grammar.

Writing is the grand stage for viewing all that is in front of you. It is a platform which allows you to notice the world for what it is. It is sometimes dramatic, comedic, and the melancholy all at once. (To observe this, is a fantastic experience every writer should look for.)

And they are telling you to find the feeling in your soul and tell the universe what it is like to witness it all so

that the world will clamor for the same feeling over and over and will continue to want more.
Emotional content is what most writing is about and your writing should be packed with it.

To bring out the emotion of the human race is what writing is. It senses, it is an emotional response, and it is excitement. It brings out the beauty of the mind's wholeness and the heart's fullness. Either writing will make you cry, or it will bring forth an anger that only you can portray in your work.

The art of writing is the ability to use your breath to express exhaustion and satisfaction simultaneously. The craft is sculpted and refined. Your words get polished to a glow which, when done properly, will attract in ways you never thought possible.

Writing is a road that few people can travel successfully. Okay, you have a book done. That's great, but where does the book go?

What kind of promotions did you have to do? What did all that cost? It is a difficult way to make a living.

A friend of mine, a publisher of a medium-sized children's imprint told me this:

"If you ever want to take a lot of money and turn it into a little bit of money, either publish a book or start a publishing firm."

He was kidding, of course, and he was telling it like it is. But the facts are the facts and whether you decide to try to get a traditional publishing deal, or you make the jump into publishing your work yourself, you must be aware of where you are venturing.

It is sort of like going hunting for a Bigfoot or thing no one has ever actually seen. They don't know how big it is, what it looks like, its smell, or for that matter its footprints.

When you are starting out on an adventure that may discourage you and drive you to quit writing altogether, try this before you go out into the industry of publishing, I highly recommend researching everything you can.

If you do not decide to dive into writing, you will have at least become knowledgeable about the publishing industry. Who knows, perhaps you will become another person who starts up a multimillion dollar online bookstore.

It can happen.

# Chapter 16-
# Chasing Fame and Fortune
### (part one)

So you want to become a well-known and famous writer, do you?

J.K. Rowling made it so you can too, right?
Stephen King made it. Michael Crichton made it. Danielle Steele, they all made it, so you figure it can't be that hard.

Wrong!!

If you have the attitude and the ignorance of looking at writing like that at the beginning of your career, you will forever be a rank amateur!

Think about it. The authors who are listed above have been at it for a minimum of 10 years. Rowling was not an overnight success. She wrote the Potter stories years before being discovered.

Danielle Steele was a writer of other topics before she made it in the adult genre she writes now.

Stephen King wrote for comic books before he got a foothold in the industry.

However, one thing that has continually helped them, and those authors who are fortunate to have their first or second or even their third book released, is good old-fashioned hard work.

The definition of hard work for all writers is-

*The act of going out and meeting people at signings in stores and libraries, special events, and speaking engagements.*
*It is the traveling, preparing and planning for an event, speech or book presentation. Doing the research to be prepared and knowing what you are preparing. Keeping your health up so you can keep going. Then having the presence of mind to sit and write more and coherently, even after being completely exhausted from an event.*

I can go on and on about the types of hard work you will have to do if you want to be successful in this business. Not to mention finding time to write on the road. Doing that is crazy making.

The time never shows up. You must force it to be there.

Recently I did a two-and-a-half-week book tour of city bookstores and a school a day. It was up to me to make sure there were books for sale at the stores and the schools, being

sure of where I was going (directions are always helpful) and keeping my stress level down.

I had to prepare for every presentation separately because they were all different. Made sure I got plenty of rest, and made sure to take care of my voice, because without that I would not be fulfilling my speaking contract. Laryngitis can be your worst enemy, but when you are tired, it gets you literally by the throat.

After all this goes on for even just a few days, it gets old fast. You get tired, cranky, and irritable; you want your teddy and a familiar bed.

But Wait! There's More!

Speaking engagements are the part new writers don't have a clue.

Signings are a beautiful thing, don't get me wrong. They are the bread and butter of your career that get you in the public eye.

When you start out as a writer, you are not known to anyone. It is up to you to find your readership. It is up to you to make your promotional flyers, table brochures, business cards, posters for your book, and get them sent out long before your appearance, so they are used for publicity in stores and schools. You will need to collect email addresses from fans. You will need to produce a newsletter and set up a social media page .

Publishers don't do this for you. They never have. That is something you have to do. Agents do not do this either. Sometimes you will get an editor that helps with promotional materials, but that rarely happens anymore. It is you who must do this. It is crucial.

Then the day of the signing arrives.
The excitement wells up inside you as you sign your first book, your second book, and so on.

You will speak with the most excellent of people, and it is you who are presenting yourself and your books and topic to the buying readers in hopes they will like you and your work. You show yourself as kind, courteous, and cordial, to everyone, and you remember to say, "Thank you!" to everyone.

But then, you occasionally get that one, uh, person, who, just because you are an author (you must be an authority, you must know everything about your subject, right?), wants to talk with you about getting published, or every aspect of your topic, because now you are an expert regarding the entire world.

They stand there in front of your table and continue to hold you and the line that is congregating in back of them, in a kind of hostage situation.
So what do you do?

The line at your signing is getting longer (something all authors should welcome), but one thoughtless person wants to endlessly pick your brain because you are, after all, an author (yes, I repeated myself) and you are, after all an authority about whatever your topic is and somehow this person relates to that. So, you must know everything there is to know about being an author and being successful.

These people who hold your line hostage, are the types of people who have no life, usually, never buy a book, and probably are there just to jabber on without thinking of anyone else or realizing there are more people in the world. So we must (short of shooting them and carrying them off), diplomatically guide them out of the way by simply saying, "Thanks for coming by." and saying, "Next." That does not always work.

Sometimes they just step aside and wait for the chance to jump back in, in front of you to keep asking questions. Normally, there is an assistant at the store event that helps with folks and keeps the line flowing.

Believe me, the "next" person will gladly step up and, through some force field will make the "annoying" person step away. So, with this new person, you write something extra special in their inscription.

Thanks for saving me! Thank God you were there to help! May your daughter marry a millionaire. Something along those lines.

Now, if the part about the person taking up the line sounds mean, it is time for a reality check.

You have worked your tail off to get to this point, and you should never let anything stand in the way of, or halt, your journey of continued success. Most of the time the last example will not happen. Most of the people you will meet will be fantastic and will be there to speak to you briefly about how much they enjoy your work, and then they will politely move on. It is those human obstacles you need to know how to get around and avoid if you can.

Both adults and children will enjoy meeting you as an author and as a real life person. It goes with the territory and the persona.

It gets even better!
The bookstore appearances are only the tip of the authorship iceberg.

The fun part is doing media appearances on radio and television shows. Getting your face and voice out on the airwaves can be a beautiful thing.

It is usually difficult to generate sales when you are not accustomed to doing it, but with media, it gives you the chance to advertise pretty much for free, where and when you will be signing your books.
Signings are great!

But there's always a catch, so, unfortunately, onto the scariest part of the whole book promotions thing: the part of getting a book published and the issue of being an author that no one knows (yet).

Your reviews can be your best friend, or they can kill your sales. However, in some cases, bad reviews have boosted sales. So here is a method (or madness), a technique for schmoozing with the newspapers and the magazine media. Schmoozing can be one of the hardest things you must do if you are to start on that trail to fame and fortune.

In the front sections of all newspapers and magazines, there is a section called the masthead. It contains all the names of all the editors and contributors for the issue you are reading. Find the editor you should be submitting the review copy to.

Research, read, and review what these editors have done in current and past issues.
Study them, and ask yourself why they gave a good or a bad review. The answer could make or break you at the bank and in the trade magazines.

The best thing you can do to gain notoriety is speak passionately about your work, and at the same time be happy and enthusiastic. Generate an energy that becomes so contagious everyone will want to talk to you. Show your readers the work and display or read (with all the dramatic force you can muster) your favorite sections.

And don't forget to tell a little of the back story of your work.

And lastly, develop a persona that says you are a special author. Not so much a gimmick, but something that tells everyone who reads your work, "This is written by an exceptional writer."

Oh, the chapter title stated a part one. There is a part two eventually, but that is something you will have to complete. Remember the efforts you place into writing will come back to you tenfold. What you put into something you will get back in a good way.

# Chapter 17-
# Apples and Oranges

Writers are a strange and unusual lot. They are the ones who find beauty in odd places, make the slightest of characters transform into a heroic persona you would have never thought possible. They put their thoughts down on paper in hopes the world will either agree with them or just simply enjoy.

But the one thing writers especially cannot get the hang of, is how to send a manuscript to a publishing editor.

There are an incredible number of new writers and would-be authors who have no grasp of the idea of the process of submitting a manuscript. It is understandable because it is not an easy thing to do. But once you have done it a few hundred times it does get easier. Mind you it is not always a successful endeavor, but at least you begin to understand.

The numerous times I have been complained to by new writers wanting to have their work considered by an editor or publishing house have always been the same complaint. "I sent them exactly what they wanted, and how they wanted it. How come the publisher did not accept my work?"

Simple, you probably did not consider the timing involved when submitting a manuscript exactly the way they instructed in the submission guidelines, or the other numerous factors in the process.

Also, there is always the research that must be done beforehand. The submission process is not a hard one. There is, however, a methodical way of getting it done correctly. Insomuch, it will not only make life easier for the acquisitions editor, whose job it is to make the decision to either keep or reject a work.

Your job as the writer is to look as professional as you can. For instance, make sure you have spelled the editor's name correctly. Nothing kills a manuscript faster than misspelling an editors name. Instantaneous death will come to an author who cannot spell. The idea is to be sure all the spelling is correct, the punctuation is as right as it can be, the formatting is as it should be. Be sure you have all the initial submission letters included.

Syntax and grammar in your query letters and proposals are necessary. They are the first items the editor will see. These are the keys to the gate you are trying to open. Everything that you have learned in  English class has suddenly become important. So hopefully, you will have retained most of it.

You must, as they say in the industry – "do the dance."

The idea that drives the dance is simple. Make it as perfect as possible when you send your child into the world for the first time.

Imagine this- You have given birth to a new story. You have taught it everything you can teach it. You have dressed it and fed it with the storyline and the polishing all stories need. But now you are ready to send the child out into the world of the publisher in hopes they will accept your little one into the fold.

You have included the letter of introduction for the teacher (editor) and it is now up to your manuscript to behave. It all stands on your shoulders. How your manuscript looks is a reflection on your abilities as a writer and the understanding you have of the publishing industry regarding the publisher's submissions guidelines.

These are the steps to the dance. You must know these entirely for each and every publishing firm you want to submit your work to. Study them and be sure you have followed them to the letter. That is why researching the details is important. The idea again is to look professional. The more professional you appear, the better your chances. I will be bringing that up again. It is important.

A topic I often explain to newbies is the one about the apples and oranges.

The problem arises when the would-be writer (as an example) writes a cookbook and sends it to a mystery publisher.

The question gets asked, "I don't understand why they rejected my cookbook."
I cannot emphasize this too many times.

---

*"Never send your apples to an orange dealer!"* T.E. Watson

---

The next question is always this one.
"But don't all publishers accept all types of manuscripts?"

I cannot get any clearer than this. No.

Some have many imprints; many different genres they handle with varying topics they prefer to work with and market. These publishers are often specialized and they do nothing else but that genre and only that genre. Whatever that is. In the instance of the big publishers in New York City, these giants have a conglomeration of many smaller publishing houses under the umbrella of one large industry corporate name.

An example that comes to mind first is Bertleman's. They own other larger publishing firms as well as many smaller, yet not less important, publishing imprints that do various genres like juvenile picture books, young adult, mystery, and what have you. It is up to you, the submitting writer, to find out where to send your apples. It is also your responsibility to show your apples only when they are ripe and ready for market.

No one likes sour or rotten apples. And no editor will read a submission if they find your work is not ready. Remember, they know their job. They can smell a rotten apple before it reaches their desk. Not that your work is a festering rotten apple, but I believe you know what I mean.

Back to the professional editor.

They are the hunting dogs, so to speak, that are in search of the bestseller for their company, and hopefully for you as well. The best way to form this a win-win is to make your child ready for the outside world entirely. Hair combed and neatly dressed, face washed, milk money in the pocket, you know what I am saying. Remember the details. Never try to submit your manuscript to a publisher that has nothing to do with your topic. It is a waste of your time and money, and it will tell the editor you are not ready for primetime. That is when the ball stops rolling for you. At least with that company.

When researching publisher information use this reference. The Writer's Market Books published by Writer's Digest. They have been in business for many years and are a reliable resource. However, if you are reading through a copy in your local library, be sure that the volume you are studying is the latest edition. If it is not, there is a good chance the information in it is not accurate and is out of date, and will cause issues if you use it. Thyey are constantly updating these volumes, so find the most recent one you can.

Buy the newest edition of the latest volume. You can also find them online.

There are numerous and different titles that Writer's Digest publishes. They produce works of many different genres and the markets that represent them. You will find tons of information in each of the topics, genres, and submission guidelines.

Each will tell you the names of editors, the departments, what the guidelines for publication are, and so on. Study this and understand it. If you follow it correctly, you have more than a good chance of getting your work published. If you have access to the internet, you can and should find the same company and see if the information in the Writer's Marketplace is the same as on the company website. Ask yourself, are the editors' names the same? Editors change so often it can be discouraging, so be extra careful when researching editor names and positions.

Are the guidelines for publication the same? Is the address the same? Have any changes to the genre or topics changed? Are the dates the same? Watch for the genre change closely. They may not publish horse stories anymore, if that is what they published. They may be publishing another entire genre. They may have started to publish books on outer space.

(Remember the apples?) If you do not do these correctly, your discouragement is your responsibility. You will have no one to blame but yourself for your lack of success with a submission.

When you get a submission back, remember it is not a personal jab at your personality or you as a human being. It is only a business message saying the firm no longer needs your kind of manuscript, they possibly have too many in their titles listing, or you need to do more homework on what they are currently asking writers to submit.

If your apples are not polished, it will show.

Just remember a rejection letter is never something that needs to be the cause of any hurt feelings. Theese letters only mean you need to work a bit harder.

Acquisition editors are the first line of defense for the publisher, or, if you want to look at them in this fashion, they are the greeter. These knowledgeable and experienced human beings sincerely want to find the literary diamond that will shine forever. They are not only helpful; they enjoy what they are doing, despite it being a difficult job. Even though they do their best, they are most times set with the hard task of sending out the rejection letters that all writers dread (if they are rookie writers). Publishing is a business after all and needs to be run in that fashion.

The editor wants to make sure their readers, who are the buyers, are not disappointed. There are so many aspects to consider in the world of the publisher, they can make your head explode, which is probably why the turnover for the position of editor, and this is correct for any publishing company, is incredible.

On average, more editors come and go every month than any other job. It is a very discouraging position and takes fortitude, and an understanding of the publishing business and editing process for a person to be a good editor and still have a good feeling about what they are performing.

Just remember these are good and ecent people behind an editors desk. When they find something the firm they work for might like, they go to bat for the author with everything in their being to get the manuscript to the next level. It is the writers job to make the editor believe in the work as much as you do.

# Chapter 18-
# Mindset

Human beings tend to look at things around them in determined and definite ways. When we do this we often make up our minds about them, and we stick to those ways. It is for no other reason than we don't know, or have never thought of, another method to our thinking.

For some reason, we often think of only one way, and that is the only way to think. A second thought never occurs to us that there might be a better mindset.
But there is one in which writers and authors need to consider.

Different thinking is often an entirely new and untraveled concept for many authors.

The one and the only way you construct your writing, whether it be submissions or whatever, has always been thought of as the way to write.

Although this may hold true in a small way, it is far from the way editors and literary agents look at your work.

New writers and experienced authors who already have several manuscripts transformed into books or magazine articles may have never thought of their writing in this way. To begin, it is feasible, you may have never been told your writing is no longer a body of work. No longer is it a storyline that took lots of time to complete.

"What do you mean it is no longer a story?"

Something magical has just happened. Your work has grown up. When your writing has grown up, is ready for real world reviewing, and, as the writer, you will find you have also transformed into a more refined and experienced writer because you are aware of the methodology and techniques of professionally presenting your work to an editor. They will appreciate it. The better you present it, the better your chances of being published.

It has transformed into a sellable product.
You, as the writer, will attempt to market and sell your product to a publisher. Then, when the time is correct, and they have accepted your product and produced it in proper book form, it is their turn to sell it to the buying readers.

It is the publisher's prerogative to sell it in any product form they wish as long as the author agrees via contract. Hopefully, the work is ready for the big time.
It is all up to you. Your product is now awaiting your decision whether you will make it a success or not.

You have seen, through various mediums, television in particular, advertisements sending a message to the buying public telling them they need the product they are hawking. All in hopes , your work is the one the publisher needs and wants for their titles listing.

When a mindset changes, it is sometimes a hard thought process for the writer to re-think the way they have always *thought* they had to do things. Since the day you could write your first words, we have listened, and everyone with any experience in the writing field said it is the way it always is done is the way to do it still. That may have been true 40 years ago, but the industry has changed for the better. Technology has had a major hand in this change. It has become easier to make a product, although the hard part is still turning the manuscript into a sellable product.

The importance of this is to make it sellable to, not only the buying public, but first of all to agents, and editors to whom are trying to sell any manuscript. If you have no idea what type of formatting you need to have for your manuscript, then find out and practice until you are well versed in the format and style.

A sellable product can take the shape of a paper-bound manuscript, or a digitally-formatted book for reading on a digital device. Both are valuable, and both have proven to be a viable way to sell your work. Each format has its audience. Digital books especially, draw a considerable market share, yet, hard copy books, both softcover, and hardcover are still the market favorites.

Everyone enjoys the feel of a book in their hands. Being able to turn a page and see on that page the world your writer's imagination has provided. Your mindset has become such an important factor, not only in the writer's process, but it has become the methodology agents and editors consider most for all new incoming manuscripts.

The mindset of an author shows in their work and the way they have presented it by following the guidelines set forth by the publisher. It is evident when a positive product mindset is apparent.

It will be advanced quicker than a manuscript package with a simple query letter and basic printed pages.

A writer's mindset and the attitude the author projects is a huge item in how their submission gets placed in the long line of the hundreds of manuscripts getting sent to editors' desks every day. It is the quest of all editors to find the diamond that needs the bit of polishing that will help display every karat proudly.

# Chapter 19-
# Machines and Style

Does the new-fangled technology among us make your writing better? Not really.
Here is a for instance.

Early on in my career, I used an old Royal typewriter I bought at a flea market for five bucks. Then I went on to what was supposed to be a more efficient electric typewriter. It wasn't. I spent more time correcting what I messed up using white out, than writing. I was not a great typist.

After a few years, the advent of word processors came to the world, which was better, but not by much.
Soon after, the machines known as computers hit the market, and everyone had to have one, despite their cost. The illusion of one of these new machines was vivid at the time.

Then, as the years passed, I paid thousands of dollars for the various models I purchased. All in hopes that somehow these mechanical and digital wonders would make my writing far better than the next hopeful writers.

It did to a point. It made it easier to stall out in mid-sentence when I was in the middle of a great line or paragraph, then I stopped and realized I was editing as I wrote.

*Dumb thing to do!*

To paraphrase, Ernest Hemingway said, "Vomit the words out onto the paper and then go back and clean it up!"

Even with all the new-fangled technologies that are among us, they do not make our writing better. They can only make it easier to see the mistakes and possibly the lack of style we have all struggled so hard to achieve.

No machine or piece of software is going to make you a great writer. It will only help get you to a point. There is no style in a machine.

I was guest lecturing at a university explaining to a student how important it is to read in order to learn style and technique. I asked a student about his reading habits and why he thought he did not need to read as part of his writing routine.

He immediately said, "I don't read because it will corrupt my writing style."

I promptly looked him the eye and told him he has no style. Yet! At least to that point. His writing was bland and lifeless, and it had no originality to it whatsoever. He needed to practice and write and study more.

My words stopped him in his tracks because he was being told by family and friends his work was good and his writing was nothing short of excellent.

Naturally, as we all do at one point or another, he believed his own hype. You know, the words of praise that close relatives and maybe a friend or two had told him.

I told him to sit down while I explained why he has no style. It sounded harsh and cold at first, but soon he started to unfold his arms and stopped scowling and shooting bullets from his eyes.

"Time to grow up," I said. "The next time you come into this class you leave your ego at the door and any pre-conceptions that others may have passed to you. You are, from here on, starting from scratch. And the first thing you are to do is to read."

I told the entire class, "A writer cannot write without knowing how and what to read. Reading will help you develop a personal style. Soon after, I heard a muffled groan.

Let's say we are all musicians. We are learning our scales, arpeggios, the three B's (Brahms, Beethoven, Bach), the difference between black keys and white keys.
Now let's say we practice our scales and arpeggios

every day, as well as the songs we have been learning. The teaching goes on for a long time, at least until the teacher says, "Alright, I have taught you all I can, and it is up to you now, to go out and put some style of your own into the compositions you have learned."

I asked them to think of a Beethoven piece turned into a jazz piece for a quartet. That's style and arrangement to the hilt. I would have liked to listen to that.

There were musicians that did turn a few of the three B's into pop hits for the radio during the 70s. Pretty good music I might add. Anyway...

Reading others' work and reading and studying the authors you like to read, both contemporary and classic, will enable you to pick up style, technique, structure, verbiage, and by some miracle of osmosis, you will gain some basic style. Not necessarily your definitive style, but a style you can explore. Eventually through this type of study you will be enabled to explore different styles and find your own.

Take H.G. Wells' *War of the Worlds,* read the book, and then see the movie. Never the other way around.
(The book is always better anyway)
You will see a difference so vast in interpretation you would wonder who wrote it first.

Each is the same story, with the styles to each of the writers' liking. Not better, just the same, and somewhat different.
How are you going to learn if not from the authors who

have a strong influence in the world of writing? You will only learn so much from an English textbook.

Learn by doing. Learn by reading, and learn by studying. Okay, now the question is why do you have to do all this to write?

You can simply put pencil to paper, with no rhyme or reason, and you can just go out and write, and the result will be dull reading. It will be writing with no style, otherwise known as beginner's writing.

No one who writes can say they do it because they are a natural writer. There is no such creature. A natural writer would not need to work hard and learn structure, style and all the rest of it. They would simply write anything that came out of their heads and it would be wonderful.

It ain't gonna happen.

To say it differently, when you read the great writers you will begin to understand what makes them tick. You will learn the times, and the era, in which they wrote. Studying the styles of other writers, especially the great writers who came before is the only way to gain a grasp of what style actually is. It is sort of like going to the grocery story, or the hardware store, or better yet the library or internet (although sometimes the internet can be misleading). If you need to find out something about something, you go to the source. If you need to find out how Ernest Hemingway wrote, you study his writing, The writing the students did in the grammatical and authors' style they preferred was a big part of how they portrayed the words they put to paper, and how the reader picked up the story and imagined it.

When you read, and analyze the great authors of all time, the creative, as well as the analytical side of your brain, will kick in. Only then will you begin to see, and fully understand, how these artists became great.

Nigel Hamilton, a famous British historian and biographer stated this regarding writing, "If your reading audience doesn't understand what you're saying, then you are talking to yourself."

If you take every story that has ever grabbed your imagination and evoked your emotions, and that story has been able to conjure up visions and places and things without any difficulty, then that writer has accomplished the goal of constructing a great piece of writing.

They have successfully made you think and become human for just a few moments. And if you never knew what it felt like before and you enjoyed the feeling, you will probably purchase more of the author's work.
You cannot begin to know what a writing style is until you have studied many of the very best. At least a few to start would be good.

If you reside in one of those categories, not only will you be ignorant you will also not be published to any noted degree. Reading is a major ingredient of writing and it must be included in a writer's life.

To read is to grasp hold of the greatest of words placed on paper. To read is to journey through Father Time's ever-changing world.

So, with all that said...

You, as the writer, forge and shape your style, you need to know how to place your particular panache and personal voice into every piece you write. Remember it has nothing to do with what type of machine you use, or what paper whiteness you prefer.

It has to do with learning from the masters. Read their works. Read the works of those who have influenced your mind in a positive or negative way. Read everything! Read things you would not usually read.

Writing is an ever-changing, ever-evolving process. Reading also changes with every new technique. Reading and writing are brother and sister.

They go hand in hand, following a well-traveled path. It is the only way we learn as writers. It is, and has been, the same for centuries.

When you read, you will find your style.
I tell my students, "There is elegance in the eloquence!"

You will never know and understand style until you have seen it in an example from one source or another. Reading, either as an enjoyment or a study tool, is never a waste of time, especially for writers.

And if you think you do not need to read, your writing will always be that of an amateur, and it will show in every piece you write.

Read out loud any Steinbeck book, especially *The Grapes of Wrath*. Read all Charles Dickens books. I recommend *Oliver Twist*, and especially Roald Dahl books. Any of them will do. Don't forget all books by Ernest Hemingway. These writing pioneers blazed trails so exact for writers today; we owe them a debt of thanks.

The writing they did in the grammatical style they preferred is a big part of how they portrayed the worlds they put to paper, and how the reader picks up the story and imagines it.

So, if you catch yourself saying, "I don't like to read because it will corrupt my writing style." You have no idea what writing style is, much less your own. You cannot even know what any writing style is until you have studied some of the very best. This process is an ongoing practice. The second you stop learning or studying this craft of writing, you will fail.

It is the only way we learn as writers. Writing has been the same for centuries. It is not about to change anytime soon.

Never stop learning.

# Chapter 20- Life or Death

Reading this could mean the difference between the life of your work or its instant death. These next three items are always the most overlooked when writers submit their manuscript. What you decide to do always dictates what happens.

Editors are continually swamped by thousands of submissions to come to their desks. Day after day there are more manuscripts than can ever be handled by mere mortals. These manuscripts have either been treated with love and compassion or are given a discretionary glimpse and then thrown into the ever-present rejection pile otherwise known as the trash bin.

The reason is, that editors, have much more to do than just reading manuscripts. Between going to production meetings with clients they are producing, meeting deadlines, trying to lay out an accurate editing job for thousands of pages of writing, and whatever else they are frantically trying to get done, they are reading your work.

These people who have the power to kill your manuscript or let it live, are human. They have emotions and feelings. They get tired and frustrated when they can't get your work done. They are caring, forthright individuals, who do their best when searching for that one manuscript which screams out saying, "I am good. Publish me!"

Editors are the experts in the field. They know how to tell when a manuscript has that special something that screams bestseller or maybe a movie production. Or, it could be or a script that needs too much work to break a sweat over.

Where am I going with this? Follow me through the wonderful world of patience. In this case, writer patience. Patience is a rare, and beautiful thing when it occurs. More new writers have blown their chances by not being patient than any other reason known to the writing world.

The last thing an editor needs is to have someone calling them up, asking the same question over and over, "What is the status of my manuscript?" Or, "Did you like it? Did you think it was good enough?"

As a writer, you will find editors, wherever they are in the chain of command, have different levels of responsibility, and different schedules to adhere to in their daily work schedule. With those responsibilities come varying levels of stress.

If you have the guts to phone an editor and take your chances of killing your writing efforts, then you are either very confident or very ignorant.

Don't let your anxiety for acceptance make you look unprofessional. If you do, you are doomed.
You must, by all means, be patient with your work as well as yourself.

An editor can smell a new writer at 50 miles. More so when the new writer does things that are held as taboo. The first of these is a personal lack of patience (there's that word again.) Don't get shook up if you don't hear from the acquisitions editor right away. Expect an average wait time of no less than six to eight months for a reply from any publishing house. This business of publishing is notoriously slow.

They are doing the best they can and as fast as they can. Go onto your next project. It will keep your mind busy, and you may improve your writing.

*More stuff: "Writing is like your body. You must exercise it to make it stronger." T.E.Watson*

The second of these taboos is not being mindful of formatting your work. Not double spacing your manuscript is the fastest way to the rubbish bin. There are no ifs, ands, or buts about it. Your blood, sweat, and ink will end their journey in the towering waste bin, never to be seen by the editor, or you again.

There are so many manuscripts on the ever-sinister rejection stack. That pile is so full it can keep a city block warm by being made part of a massive fireplace.

Remember to double check your details. To be considered a professional it must look as if you (at least) know what the game is about; even if you have never published before.

There are thousands of new writers who have never been published, but they keep trying. They do this by the improvement of their work in the way it is laid out in its first impression. The first impression being the first thing the editor sees when they open that envelope.

Make sure the title is clean, clear, and not splotched out. (Inkjet cartridges sometimes do that.) Do not make hand corrections. Do not use whiteout. Include a cover letter. Learn how to write one.

Let the editor know with whom they are potentially working. Just a little information, not your entire life story. Tell what the book is about in a short four-line description. And most of all, be polite.
Do not become a know-it-all.

Editors will not look at you twice or consider even giving you a chance if you feel you know more than they do. They have no time for nonsense.

Remember this is what they do on a daily basis, and they know what they are doing. NEVER second-guess an editor.

They, in the best scenario, try to make a win-win situation for everyone.

The acquisitions editor at a publisher is the first editor that will see your work. They are usually very overwhelmed and very busy. If you want this to be a win-win situation between the acquisition editor and yourself and your writing, then patience is of the utmost importance at this stage in the game.

When sending the query letter or proposal, it is critical you understand what these are. You need to look into different aspects of them or ask somebody who's been in business for any number of years to find out how to really and successfully construct a query letter or a proposal letter. Writing those types of inquiries are vital to just getting in the door of any publishing house. It takes practice. It takes lots of practice.

Package your manuscript well. Make it look professional. And always include an SASE if required. (Self Addressed Stamped Envelope). It is still a good idea to do this, either by e-submission or hard copy query letter. Be sure that you have practiced and understood how to write a query letter so your editor will appreciate you are trying to be as professional as you possibly can. Not sending an SASE will guarantee a quick trip to the trash can.

*Remember: Always double space your work. It is easier for the editor to read and much more pleasant to mentally digest. It will get back to you faster, and your anxiety level will drop considerably.*

These are the last of the nightmares which should be avoided. Formatting incorrectly is the ghastliest of the mistakes writers do. There are useful formats that are acceptable, but this is about what not to do.

Never send a manuscript that is hand-written. In this age of computers, word processors, and other means of typesetting, there is no excuse for sloppy work. If you cannot do this, find someone who can and if need be pay them.

Even in the outermost region of the Antarctic, there are typewriters. If you are to be considered a professional, you must take the time to find at least a typewriter or someone who has one. Laziness is never acceptable.

Don't be in such a hurry that it jeopardizes your chances to be a literary discovery. Nothing done in haste is done well. Take the time to do it right. When a manuscript is hand-written, then submitted, it has a short life. Don't do this to yourself. There is enough rejection out there. You should want to send a manuscript that not only makes you feel good about sending it; that makes the editor feel good about receiving and reading it.

You must make yourself and your work bulletproof to the editor's blue pen or red pencil in many cases. You should check and recheck every nook and cranny of the work before you send it.

There have been thousands of times authors have sent works and then thought there was a better way to format it. Or they have sent it and gone through the stomach wrenching feeling that they left something out. That feeling of being unsure is a killer. Self-doubt will get you if you do not take the time to check your work. Sloppy work will keep you in the muck of the unpublished. Keep checking it until you are 120% sure.

By no means are all writers successfully being published. It is astonishing to imagine the number of wannabe writers who are hoping to become authors. It is very overwhelming to try to absorb them all. However, you are at a good starting point.

Remember these items:

When submitting your work, keep your work clean and double spaced.

Check and recheck. If you find something that needs polish, do it immediately after you have looked into what looks like it needs some correction.

Keep in mind the editors are people too, and they do have an enormous amount of work to do every day. They need to be able to consider every manuscript equally. Your manuscript is not the only work they have to read.

They are looking for that special manuscript that will be a possible bestseller. The one that can sell books for the publishing firm, and you the author.

Take the time to do it right. Never send in something that will drive you crazy wondering if it was less than perfect.

# Chapter 21-

# The Power of the Writer Memory

I t has been said writers and comedians have the most amazing memories. It has also been studied and verified by scientists in several major colleges specializing in brain and mind function, to be true (MIT, Stanford Medical College, and Oxford Medical University).

The strange ability to remember things from times past is truly a phenomenon that has yet to be understood fully.

In the case of writers, it is a blessing. This ability to recall some odd and strange memories is remarkable. Most writers have this ability to recollect things of all sorts. They remember old television programs, yet having never viewed them, they have no idea where they got the information. Writers tend to remember dates and times with surprising accuracy. The wheres and whens of medical issues like that of a vaccine when they were a child and even an infant.

People ask me things who want to know answers to some of the most obscure topics, and I have been able to answer without being entirely sure how I know the information. I confidently supplied the correct answer to the question. It is something none of us understand but enjoy having at our disposal. It is almost as if we are on a quiz show and not getting a single answer wrong.

However, that does not always happen for every topic. We don't know if it is because we research a great deal, or if it is due to some physical transformative brain function of some sort. Although it does not, or has not caused any of us any physical or emotional pain, we tend to go along with this power of the mind quite often, and I do mean every day. If we need something, we somehow bring it up from the files in the backs of our brains and can use it. Where those cabinets of files came from is a mystery to us, but we use them, and we are happy they are there.

These items writers bring up are usually pieces of other things that possibly had some effect on us at some point in our lives. Or, in the case of myself, I remember things I should not know anything about but do.

For instance, I can be watching a television program from the fifties, long before I was thought of, and tell you who an actor is and what and where an actor's career went after they left a show. Our family never owned a TV until I was a much older kid. I never watched TV at a friend's house. I did not know what TV was until I was almost 12 years old, and then I was only allowed to view it for a short few hours per week. As a kid I went to movies on Saturday afternoons for 75 cents which included popcorn and drink, and that was it for viewing anything on a screen. The trailers, the previews and the cartoons of which there were usually no less than six. Then the main feature. Not a bad way to use up a Saturday for a kid.

These movies were mostly the B-type of sci-fi films that all young kids liked to watch. I can tell you all kinds of things about the theater, the snack counter, even the way the front entry way was designed and decorated.

It is weird how my memory works, but I am glad it is there.

I still question why I have this gift of memory. I can still remember the telephone number of my childhood home, including the area code. I digress.

The greatest aspect of having a memory like this is the massive resource library of events and characteristics of places, people, and things. I can ask my writer mind something and voila', there it is in living color for me to take what I need.

Writers can remember people and the conversations they had, the situations that brought about the conditions of a crime or an accident. What color something was in detail, and so on.

Our memories are, as they say in comic books, are used for good instead of evil. But there is one thing that is sacrificed in having a great memory. Personally, I have a difficult time remembering the names of adults. I can remember the names of children and animals, but adults completely throw me. Now I know many adults, and I know their names well and always will, so don't get me wrong.

Even after doing a book signing, children who come to get a book signed I will remember, but their parents' names are a chore. I can only suppose some part of my memory is on vacation.

We use these memory super powers to describe items in stories. Characters in full regalia, even crime scenes.

Often down to the smell of a city alley, the aroma of garbage cans, and the sounds and types of sirens rushing down a city street. Is it an ambulance or a fire truck, or perhaps a police car? Sirens are different all over the U.S.A. So how do we know? We don't really, we just do it without thinking about it.

The use of memory can be and does scare some of us, due to this fact, we do not know where we got the information with any validity. It makes no sense to have a somewhat photographic memory and not know where the information came from. When you are a small child, I mean just months old, it is thought you have no tangible memory abilities at all. It is turning out to be an entirely false concept.

This research is a new idea process, even more so with small infants. It is the type of study that is checked only by the assistance of an electroencephalogram (EEG) or an MRI machine. It's hard to produce any results which are definable at that age.

Where does this leave us as writers? Where did we get the incredible powers of memory? Were we blessed with great powers of observation? We don't know.

Perhaps the question should be, do we care where it came from as long as we can use it and have it be there to help us keep writing?

I'll vote for the latter. You can keep your MRI machines and just let me write.

# Chapter 22- Competition

The world of publishing is a highly competitive industry. When people say, every book has its reader, unfortunately, some books do not find a reader. In some instances, the book sits in obscurity never to be read because the author has not done their promotions and gotten the title out into the world.

There are great people working in the firms that line Hudson Street in New York City, don't get me wrong. But when it comes to fighting for the life of your book, it is the author who must defend it at all costs for it to survive in the marketplace.

If you are one of the adventurers who has dabbled in the world of self-publishing, you must do this with even more fervor. The competition is hiding in the nooks and crannies of the unexpected.

They live in the bookshelves of book and gift stores.
If you plan on selling your book to major chain bookstores, you will find it difficult and somewhat impossible. Most stores will not stock them unless you have the credibility to have your book inserted into the bookstore corporate buying system. That is quite the ordeal and is a time taker.

The average length of time it takes to get a book accepted and placed within a store's retail system can take as long as eighteen months. That is just the acceptance process. It is the nature of the beast. The process of getting books into a distribution warehouse is altogether different.

Wholesalers are the middlemen that sell the books they get from the publishers. Retail stores don't buy at retail, they get books at a discounted price or on a consignment basis. Approximately little more than 55 percent is what the wholesaler's take is. You get what is left over, which is usually not much. But wait, there's more!

So back to the distributors. These are the businesses that ship books to the retailers. They too, take a big chunk of what's left of your cake. Every time a middleman takes a percentage, that is less money for you, the author.
This figure also varies from distributor to distributor.
There is no standard.

Crazy business, right? How can anyone or any company make money with so many fingers in the cake?
Many small to medium publishers now prefer not to deal with any wholesalers or distributors, due to the overwhelming percentages they take, so they sell directly to stores.

It was a great way to do business in the early days, and it still is today. So if you are planning to do business with a small to medium publisher ask them how they plan to distribute your titles, and to what wholesalers, if any, they use to get your books into stores. The wholesale and the distribution was at one time all taken care of by the publisher. There is no reason they cannot handle that now.

Do you understand why I said they are unnecessary?
In the beginnings of the publishing industry of the twentieth century, people bought books direct from the publisher. There was less hassle, more order accuracy, no sharing the pie, and the publisher had no returns. The author would receive a real monetary gain, and everyone ended up happy.

These two middlemen operations, in my opinion, are the reason the industry is screwed up. If you are a self-published independent author, you would have all the control regarding how you sell your books and to whom they are selling.

Control is a good thing. However, you must keep track of everything, including costs, overhead, and inventory, just like the big boys.

Let's get back to the competition aspect of the industry.

One of the best examples is the children's book industry. There were over three hundred thousand books published just in the United States of America in 2016.
Not to mention other countries like China who out published every country on the planet.

These numbers do not include self-published books.
So, your odds of having competition and being another's competition are sky high. If selling a book was simple there would only be two books on any subject, but there are not.

Go into any sizeable bookstore and look at the sections. Each one is different, and each one has so many titles it is hard to count the books on the shelves.

Go into the children's section of your favorite big name bookstore, for example, and look at the thousands of titles. No author can say they don't have competition. Every book on every shelf is vying for purchase dollars. The books are sorted and categorized by subject, or author, or publisher.

Stores have used this method for years.

The reason being is this, promotions.

The more money a publisher is willing to put into the promotions of a book the better the chances the book has of selling and surviving the remainders shipped back to you. Publishers do not place a whole lot in promotional budgets these days.

The only time a promotional budget is considered is when the book is written by a best-selling author who has a proven track record.

Then it may only be a dollar per book per the size of the book run. If the book has a run of 10,000, then there may be a $10,000 promotional budget. Book promotions are done primarily by larger publishing houses. Smaller publishers cannot go anywhere near that figure, so they do not do much. The budget does not go far. There are industry and trade magazines who charge large amounts of money for ad fees. One ad can go for thousands.

For instance, a one-time insert in an issue of a particular magazine with the initials of PW, a major trade magazine, considered to be the bible of the publishing industry, and there goes your promotions budget.

This is not necessarily a bad idea, but because of the numerous other adverts for other books yours may or may not get seen. It is a risky gamble and something to consider.

You may notice many of the books on a shelf are sorted by publisher. The potential of that book being seen by the customer is figured out early on in production and the more promotional budget there may be for that publisher's titles.

Bookstore shelf space is expensive. Publishing houses rent real estate in bookstores. The shelves are that expensive in-store real estate. The bigger the publishing house, the more real estate they occupy. And, if you notice what are called end caps, in stores, they are the prime real estate and are ridiculously costly for a book publisher to place titles on them, and that is only temporary. That is how bookstores make their money.

As far as competition goes, the budgetary promotional money involved with any book is minimal, thereby making it necessary to compete against other books on the shelves. You can ill afford to let your book just sit waiting for someone to buy it. It is like sitting alone in the desert waiting for someone to bring water.

You can be nice to someone all you like, but if they have a book similar to yours, you have no choice but to sell your heart out to be sure your book outsells theirs.

You do not need to be unfriendly about any of it. When you're talking up your book, remember to keep a good attitude about you.

A pleasant demeanor is important when hawking your title. You are talking with people, not buyers. Keep it friendly and stay calm when a customer walks away without buying from you. Thank them for their time and consideration and hope to see them again soon.

They may not have been able to purchase right then.

They may have already bought your books somewhere else. There are many reasons. Not buying is not a personal jab at you or your work. Just remember you are there to promote your work, customers purchasing is an extra slice of pie. If they don't buy it's okay.

Self-published authors have even more work to do. You are footing the bill for all of it: the book production, the promotional materials, the shipping costs, editing, etc. And now many book retailers will not stock even a few independent book titles so you have even more work to do. These are all the content and building blocks of your project. Most of all, you need to know how to sell your work. In this case, promotional materials are essential. They are a simple and inexpensive method to help keep your name on the tip of the fingers and tongue.

Before they leave your display or table, hand them a bookmark or business card. If you have them, give them your brochure. All these are items that can be had for a song. Easy to design and easy to order via the various printing firms on the internet. When you the author are doing every job in publishing, if that is what you prefer, you must know how to do these things, or at the very least have knowledge of what they entail.

Designing is a cheap method if you do things yourself. Designing well is another subject. Don't assume you can just go out and say you are a designer. There are certain artistic rules and training that need to be applied, and if you don't follow them, you will have wasted lots of time. Time is something you cannot afford to lose. If you have a poorly designed book it will not sell. It will look amateurish and it will be alone on a shelf for many days.

But most of all, know how to search for deals in printing both your books and your promotional materials.

Don't be satisfied with something that looks okay. The idea is to strive for as great as you can get.

Then get to know where you can get the best deal on your ISBN numbers, your bar codes for the back of your book, where to get a bio photo head shot, and who is best to design a book cover. The list goes on.

All of it is another reason to be sure you stand out from the crowd when it comes to selling your book. Figuratively speaking, your book must know how to jump up and down to get attention, and you must know the ropes to help it along. Competition in the book world? Oh, yes, it exists. Anyone who says it doesn't is fooling themselves.

Many people want to be considered nice and help other author's make it, are taking valuable time away from their own books and doing an injustice to the hard work and time they placed into their own work. The idea of getting a book out into the world for people to read is what this business is about, and that means ahead of the masses that also want the same.

Just because companies publish books one year and the books are not successful, does mean they may stop publishing books the next, due to monetary output.

It is a crazy, expensive industry for the projected outcome. Self-publishing normal folk don't usually have upwards of twenty thousand dollars to throw at a book that may not succeed. It is difficult to try to research a book beforehand. The book industry is a luxurious crap shoot.

Books are the dice you roll. You can never know how the dice are going to come up.

However, remember, there are publishers that will continue, thereby increasing the number of books competing for buying dollars. Ask yourself this: If the odds are not in your favor from the start, do you keep at it, no matter your odds?

Book publishers look to find the diamond in the rough. The one that is so incredible almost everyone will read it.

Strive for that book. Is it yours?

# Chapter 23-

## War Makes Strange and Dynamic Writing

Throughout the history of man as a race of beings, there has been the unique need to have major conflicts between cultures and civilizations.

The so-called desire to overcome an opposing society, take lands that are theoretically required by the imposing culture, or even because one man's girlfriend was the most beautiful ever seen to that point in history, such was the case in the Trojan war. Helen was her name, and she was supposed to be the most beautiful woman to have ever lived.

Further on in history, man saw fit to chronicle his deeds of destruction. His endeavors to overcome and try to ultimately convince the other side that their way was the only way, and if they did not believe in the same way, they were doomed for all eternity.

Religious wars, for instance, have been the cause of many lives lost unnecessarily. But there are several things in which recording the events of war have in common. You can find them in every novel, every first-hand account, and every memory of a battle.

Each of the greatest books including, *A Farewell to Arms* (Hemingway). *War and Peace* (Tolstoy), *The Red Badge of Courage* (Crane), and even *Catch 22* (by Joseph Heller), and *Mash* (by Richard Hooker), some less than others, but all have these commonalities.

When war is chronicled, the whole aspect of death and blood and guts is just the surface of the subject. The real themes to the stories are the human events, hand in hand with emotional content.

Emotional content is the backbone of every great war story, or any type of story. Whether it makes you laugh, cry, feel hatred, make you question the reason the story you are reading came to begin.

It is this emotional content that tells the stories of every character, why every event happens, and what happens to the lives of those involved, why they are affected and in what ways.

Writing about war is not just about the soldiers and a belief so strong they are willing to make the ultimate sacrifice. It also includes families, mothers, fathers, aunts, uncles, grandparents, brothers. sisters, girlfriends, and don't forget wives. It is all about the living human experience.

A war story includes the political undertones that often include many of the reasons the war is happening.

This conflict you are reading about involves more emotions than most stories. Betrayal, loss, sadness, pride, confusion, and anxiety, are just a few of the numerous types of feelings the human condition carries within the pages of the story. The firing of bullets and artillery, the feelings of fear, not only the soldiers on the side of what would seem the good guys with the white hats but the bad guys with the black hats as well.

Historical war books, the ones that give those non-fictional facts from the first hand of the soldiers who lived through a conflict, police action, or all-out war, are the ones to glean the most information.

These help the fiction writer be able to include actual types of accounts in your work. It is researched and becomes a well-read story.

On the other side of the writing coin, writers are always in search of the perfect story. But since there has never been a perfect war, a perfect story, or in this case, the greatest war story, will never exist.

It has never been written, and I do not think ever will. Remember, history is written by the winners. Is it up to us to write it albeit unpleasant?

It is our duty as writers to write any actual truth and not some modern media's rendition or opinionated version.

Also, remember that although war is one of the most destructive forces on earth it has also been one of the most precise teachers.

If we are not to relive the mistakes of our past, we must remember our true history.

# Chapter 24- Never Let Your Mother Read Your Work

A new writer asked me, "Is it okay to have my mom look at the work I just finished? I wanted to have her edit it and check it for mistakes." I went silent. Mainly because I was hoping they did not say that.
I think there should be an editing law that states – Never Let Your Mother Look At Your Work. Period!

And this is the reason- unless your relative is an accomplished professional editor, you may as well have just torn up the hours you put into your work. Your mom or other relative says," It's nice dear." You will naturally want to believe them and think it must be okay. Then you keep going on empty words that have no real meaning when it comes to your project.

What does "It's nice dear," mean anyhow?
Ask the question to see if they did read the story.

If they stammer when they say they read your work, then I rest my case .

Why?

It is because common sense must dictate here.
Try to think of the situation this way.

Let's say you are sick and need major surgery on your heart. You are prepped for the surgery and given the anesthesia, wheeled into the operating room, and then a person who looks to be a surgeon comes in.
They hopefully will be able to fix your problem, but it turns out what appears to be a doctor is a person only dressed in scrubs, and has no medical experience whatsoever.

Then the person says, "I am only here to clean the floor."
They are not a surgeon.
Scary huh?

Do you want someone who has no knowledge of what to do or how to do it, do the job? Do you want an untrained person, who is not qualified to do a job that should be performed correctly by a trained person with experience? Or would you rather have your Mom look at your work and tell you it's nice?

Yes, this sounds cold but, to make your work stand out from the crowd, you must have it looked over by a professional editor.

It will probably cost some money, but it will be worth it. Professional editors are worth every cent.

Editors will know everything they need to make your writing better than you thought it could be. Most editors will correct and define without changing your voice. A good editor will tell you where to polish and why to polish.

The paragraphs that are weak and need help will look far better with the assistance of a refined editorial review.

A bad editor will only do what they know to do and that is edit badly. They will not know the different editing style platforms, such as Chicago, AP, and several others.

No matter what type of writing or whose writing it may be, pro or amateur, it will be made to read easier than before with an editor's guidance.

There are four main types of editing.

Copy-editing is done primarily during a final or finishing point of a manuscript before publishing.

Proofing or Proof-Reading is somewhat the same as copy-editing. Proofing is when the work is corrected. Proofreaders take a pencil and place what are called proofreader's marks on the manuscript.

These resemble shorthand, and unless you know the marks and their meanings, you will need a cheat sheet to determine what they are, but well worth having.

The sheet will also help you know what you need to do to improve the work.

Some, but not all, of the proofing done today is done on computers as opposed to the proofreader's marks in pencil. Most is still done by hand as the editor reads the writing.

Substantive editing is another type. Editing this way is a process of rewriting the manuscript. It is particularly specialized. The goal is to change the wording without changing the author's voice.

Developmental editing is the meeting of minds.
The editor works with the author right from the start. They develop the idea from the beginning to the end. Developmental editing is done typically with book projects, but not always.

Now, if you have read to the chapter about where to place your ego before you start a new project, you will understand this.

The ego is dangerous. It has a life of its own and, more often than not, it makes a person look downright foolish. In the case of a writer submitting for the first time, they cannot afford to be seen in that light. Unless of course you only want to be looked at as a hobbyist.

But in the case of the potential writer as a professional, then take notes and pay close attention to what your editor says. Do not even think you know more than they.

Most editors will have been doing it for a long time if they are of any worth. The editors at large traditional publishing firms know when someone is going to be a cocky new writer and is going to give any grief.

The attitude of the new writer is something most editors know well. They can tell if they can immediately toss the work and reject it, even though it may be pretty good.

An editor can tell when a newbie is going to have an air of "I know more than you. I wrote it after all."
The holier than thou attitude is a certain death knell for a new writer. Editors have no time to jostle with someone who has no clue about the needs of the editor regarding a work.

To an editor, it becomes apparent this newbie writer is, and will probably be, an amateur for a long time, if not forever.

Not all amateurs have bad attitudes. Most do not, but there are those who let their ego come forward and lead them on the path to destruction, never to be heard from again. Possibly that is where they were headed anyway. A bad attitude will kill a writer's attempted career so fast it would make your head spin off your neck. You may as well have never taken up the task of trying to write any major work.

As for the writer, whose ego has been kept in check it does not mean the work is terrible. It just means the work is not right for the titles list of the company.

It is so important to make a great first impression, either personally or via mails; the first impression can either build you up or tear you down.

Every editor wants to do their best. Not only because they want to find a great new book for the publishing firm, but they want to be sure that everyone, including the author, is happy. A win—win is what it is all about for the editor.

If they cannot do their job, they do not last long in the publishing industry.

An editor's employment term is often not very long. The editors at the starting position are changed so often, when you just get to know one they are usually let go or they resign.
It is a difficult way to make a living.

# PART 2-
# STONE

# Chapter 25-

# The Ergonomic Writer

For those who have never heard the term ergonomics, here is what it is and why it is important to writers.

*It is the study of peoples efficiency in the working environment.*

Writers seldom pay attention to this. These are a few items that will help a writer's productivity.

*Breathing.*
It is a physical thing we do every day of our lives. It is also a vital part of the well-being of a writer's ability to create. Without oxygen, we tend to nod off. Sometimes, we do this on our keyboards, whereby we awake with a screen filled with the letters our head has landed on. Strange but true. More manuscripts disappear because of the occasional nap on a keyboard than you can imagine. The ergonomics of writing and just sitting at your desk is critical to the creative process; it is paramount that we remember to do the simple act of breathing.

It is not always automatic. Many times, I have found myself not breathing, thereby with the droopy eye-lidded feeling of being tired, I drop off the face of the world and promptly forget the words I was crafting. And when I awaken, the first word out of my mouth is "crap!" Then I try to recover what I was writing or at least thinking about, usually to no avail. But how does anyone forget to breathe? Quite simply. As writers, we tend to get so deep into our work we even forget or neglect to eat. I am famous for that.

"Honey, dinner is ready."
"Okay I will be right there, just gotta finish this paragraph."
Five minutes later, same thing. Then ten minutes, then 20, and so on, until I end up having to reheat the food in the microwave a couple of hours later.

*Getting back to breathing-*
Breathing is similar. We don't usually wait to breathe. We do tend to breathe in a more shallow fashion if our posture is not corrected. That does not allow oxygen to our brains or the rest of us to help us keep the blood flowing into our minds, which keeps us creating, which makes it possible to do great work, and I think you get the idea. So do what all writers should do, but don't.

Be conscious of your functioning body.
Breathe. Go outside and stretch. Take a short walk, play with your kids or the dog, play basketball, do whatever. Just get some new air into your lungs and your system. The more you become aware of your physical habits, the better your concentration will become.
Now go back inside and write great things.

*Office Chairs–*

The next topic brings me to the ever-present crummy chair where most of you sit. Chairs are the single most reason we do not breathe properly. Our seats are too short in the length of thigh, or not high enough, and most essentially the backrest is not adequate and causes our spine to scream at us.

Not everyone can afford an expensive office chair. There are some pretty expensive ones out there. But this is the one thing that often dictates how well and how long we work at our desk. Working comfort is important. If you are not comfortable, you will know it, and your writing will suffer. Buying an office chair is not something where you just walk into an office supply store and say, "I'll take that one." To choose an ergonomic seat takes time. It can take as long as one hour per each chair you try out.

You need to sit and feel and get into odd positions writers find themselves. Stand up and see how your back and legs feel after sitting for a time. Ask yourself, are my legs asleep or are my feet tingling? How are your arms and hands? Have you noticed where your hands and forearms rest on the arms ( if it has arms) of the chair? Your shoulders are just as important in this evaluation. One other important thing I must not leave out. Make sure it has enough leg room for yourself and enough lap room for your cat.

Your upper body is connected, and you need be aware of how all of it is reacting to the chair you just tried out. Most of all, are you tired after resting for a short time? Shopping for a chair can take several hours, days, or a couple of months. Being comfortable is well worth a careful decision.

*Computer mice-*
A more important item you will never pick. Most office supply stores have displays of various brands and designs to choose. These displays allow you to try the mice out and show you how each reacts to clicking commands. Be mindful of how your hand feels while resting on the top of the mouse. Not everyone's hands fit a mouse's engineered design, and after a few minutes begin to hurt and feel sore. Look for a double button mouse with a scroll wheel and feel how your fingers are a few moments of using the secondary mouse button. You should do this process for trackball mice as well. These are harder on many hands, but many users swear by them. It is your choice, and it all depends on how your hand feels afterward.

*The Way You Sit–*
After you consider your health and how much time you have lost because of the aches and pains you experience when sitting at your desk now is the time to look at the way you are sitting.

When sitting at your desk, it is important to keep aware of how your posture is. You may need to retrain yourself in the way you sit. Do you sit straight? Do you slouch? Are you hunched over? If you are not lucky enough to have a chair with an adjustable back for lower back support or even middle back support, you must take care to get up and stretch at least once an hour. I am not speaking of hardcore exercise.

There are a few things to keep limber and maintain the blood flowing in your spine and the overall core of your body.

Doing these few small exercises will keep you breathing. I recommend shoulder rolls, shoulder shrugs, a few leg lifts, rotate your ankles a few times, toe touches (do the best you can) are always right to loosen the back, and perhaps a couple of side-to-side stretches.

### *Your Hands and Fingers–*

Do not crack your knuckles. Knuckle cracking does nothing for your fingers. Some say differently. If you find that it is good for you then go for it. The fingers are an intricate mechanical part of the human structure and if you are a knuckle cracker you could be doing some serious damage. Especially if you are prone to arthritis and other ailments like that.

Do this instead- using fingertips, very gently place the fingers on the edge of your desk and slowly stretch downward until you feel a slight pull on the middle of your hand, then release. Take a few seconds to wiggle your fingers and shake your hands out.

Doing this will help to relax them and bring some well-deserved blood flow back into them.

Your writing pen is an implement many writers take for granted. It either works for you or it doesn't. It can make your handwriting elegant or make it look like scribbles. It took me about a hundred dollars and much experimentation to find a pen that would not kill my hand after writing out the first draft of a news story or would not make my hand writhe in pain after autographing hundreds of books for fans. All of whom wanted a personalized saying just for their special friend. A good pen or pencil is vital to the health of your fingers, wrists, and hands overall. Arthritis is more common in all of us these days, but having a tool that can help us avoid it should be something we carefully examine. Everyone's hands are different in shape size, grip, and condition. The hand is a marvelous mechanical wonder and is damaged easily due to overuse, therefore making a proper fitting pen essential.

It is something to keep in mind.

Technology is wonderful. Even though technology has provided us with the availability of computer dictation, it is not always accurate. Not every writer understands the method behind the function when using it. For instance, remembering to say the type of punctuation in a sentence or at the end, as in saying the word period, comma, or question mark, when needed for a sentence. If you do not say them, the dictation application will not place them in, leaving it to look unfinished and awkward to read.

*Our Eyes–*
One of the most important, if not *the most* important, physical aspects a writer uses every second of the day is our eyes. Without them, we would never be at our peaks as writers. As they are an essential pair of operational visual machines, they are the marvel that helps us with understanding not only what we are writing, but gives us the methods to use our remaining senses. Each of the other sense properties is enhanced when using our eyes. A good natural lamp is the best friend your eyesight can have. Never depend on the back light from a computer screen. It is nowhere near enough to provide you with a source that will not strain

your eyes. Strained eyes will become tired and painful.
A good lamp will cost as little as 50 bucks from a local big
box hardware store or art supply store. They are a good value
for the money, as the light bulb usually lasts for many years.
And as always, the newest technology often makes things
less expensive. The best way to shop for one of these lamps
is to look at it while turned on. Does it strain or hurt your
eyes? Do they make your eyes feel dried out after a few
seconds? Do you need to rub your eyes to bring them back
to life? (other than having dry eyes to begin with)

If any of this occurs, then the lamp you are looking at is not
right for you. I always recommend a natural bulb type light.
They are not cheap, but they are well worth the investment.
Your eyes will thank you, and you will be able to write for
longer periods of time.
Breathe some more-
Now, getting back to the actual act of breathing. We take
breathing for granted. We do it naturally, and we tend to
forget that we are breathing at all.

This exercise will not only help you process the oxygen, but
will increase the air that is inhaled so your body can use it
more efficiently.

You can do this either standing up and or sitting.
Find a place of quiet for a few minutes. Close your eyes
and place your opened right hand over the middle of your
chest, then put your left hand over your right hand. Your
eyes should remain closed. With your eyes gently closed and
your hands placed on your chest, breathe slowly in through
your nose and out through your mouth. Gently brethe in

and breathe out a few times.
Do this three times and only three. Any more than three
is not needed.

Open your eyes and breathe gently one more time.
Bring your hands and arms to your side and breathe
deeply one more time and let it out through you
mouth. You will be ready to start writing again.

Using these methods are not harmful if you take things
slowly and gently. Use them wisely. Having used them for
years, these are techniques that have proven themselves.

If you are experiencing some sort of health issue beforehand
be sure to see your health care provider before doing any
sort of exercise.

# Chapter 26- Pushing Swings

At some time as children, we experienced the joy of being launched upward into the air as we sat on a playground swing hanging onto chain, or rope handles by our parents, or someone who would push us safely with little drama. With perhaps a bit of the feeling you get when riding a roller coaster. They would direct us higher and higher, closer and closer, our toes targeted to the clouds trying to touch each wispy strand.

Each push made us giggle and smile knowing that something new was about to happen with every carefully controlled launch into the air. We sat awaiting a new adventure secure in the knowledge that we would enjoy the ride. And when the journey ended, terra firma would be there to greet us as we came to a complete stop.

This is a great memory, but what does this have to do with writing?

What I just described is what your reader experiences with you, as the storyteller/writer/author, at the helm of their imaginations. It does not matter what genre you are guiding them through, or what type of story line. What does matter is you have taken control of their worlds, temporarily, and with their permission, to bring suspense, joy, anger, glee, sadness, fear. You can name any emotion, and that is what they have asked you to help them experience.

Let's look at this in another way.
Your reader hops into the swing and is ready to fly. (They have opened your book, for example.) You are at the helm of this literary journey, and you are the captain of this flight. Your reader is the passenger. You, as the author, are the one doing the pushing.

With each beginning page, every word on this page starts out with a slow and building plot. It sets the scene, the main character, and possibly the antagonist as well.

The swing starts to gain a little momentum. (You are pushing gently, to begin with.) You are pushing a bit harder and with more intensity, until the reader is in the air fully engulfed in the storyline.

With you controlling the ride of the imagination, and this journey with your words, you have full ability to either make your reader feel fulfilled or come away empty after they climb off the swing. If they are enjoying the time on the swing and want to go up and up, then the reader will continue reading. Even if the book is making them fall into the depths of despair right alongside the main character. It has made them feel! Feeling the story or character is most of what writing fiction is.

Readers want that attraction, that attachment of emotion. They need personal involvement with the story. They want to feel they could help the character or the situation, if they could only be right there with sword in hand or to be in the crowd doing their best to tell that the pig is unique, or the pirate was not all that bad.

Every writer must examine their ability to bring out emotion from their words and sentences. This skill includes even how-to books. The reader, in this case, wants to have some amount of success, in which they can feel they have, usually and in most cases, a feeling of happiness from the task they have completed. Whether it is doing a craft of some sort, or self-help; to be able to be triumphant in the goal they have set is also a success for the author.

It is vital to find a good emotions chart as a reference. One that will not only show you the first emotion but one that will expand the listing of the first emotion and give you more defined ways of writing the feeling.

Finding the real emotion, not just the right one, is the goal. The right one could be anything and go anywhere and completely confuse your character as well as your reader. The correct emotion, for instance; when representing fear, or any variant of sensory emotion, such as accelerated heart rate (okay that's not an emotion), a shaky voice, (well neither is that one). Fear in itself is an emotion. It says something intimidating has occurred and there is a conflict, although possibly a slight certainty, a life could be lost, or a hidden door which has never opened for a time suddenly discovered. A character does not know what is on the other side. With lights dimmed, it's getting dark outside making it harder to see clearly or at all. Your character imagination begins to rev up to a frenzy of what possibly could be behind that door. The unknown is a good way of bringing forth the use of the fear emotion in characters.

Showing sadness takes many forms. It can be crying, a face frowning, even whimpering. When a character is sad, they go through many versions of sorrow. Depression, a sudden quietness in demeanor, the single tear rolling down a cheek. The character's eyebrows lift while the rest of the face has dropped to a puddle of worry.

When a writer can remember the emotions they have experienced and the ways they experienced them, it will be relatable to the reader. The world has not changed much when it comes to emotions and human beings. It is and always will be a continuous flow.

The senses we bring into a story line are vital. No matter how many or how often. Happiness, sadness, anger, impatience. All are critical to the livelihood of any character. Without the emotional appeal of characters, they are not real to the reader. Characters must possess the same senses we all have. Writing must be something the reader can or has felt at one point in their lives unless they have never known pain or happiness and have excused themselves from earth.

In your role as writer, you must know exactly when to use emotional interjection. Or, in this case, when and how to push your reader's swing, giving the reader a feeling of elation. And then how to keep sadness away while keeping them from falling.

# Chapter 27-

# Characters Are Born from Within

With Special Thanks to Ernest Hemingway

There are times when you will do a speaking engagement when you get asked where you get the ideas for the characters in books. After that, you might say you dream them up.

That will not be entirely correct. For instance, I may put all the characteristics of different people I've seen into one big pot of soup and then spill it out onto the table and see who or what comes to the top.

Comedians and writers are the best observers of the world. Both need to keep up with the latest and greatest of all things going on. The performer uses his powers of observation to gather the information of the times.

A writer does much the same and more.

As writers, we must take our powers of observation to a different level, to a more detailed elevation.

Many of the great writers of the past, Mark Twain, Robert Louis Stevenson, and H.G. Wells, to name but a few, wrote these details into forms that have come to be known as character sketches, and from those character layouts, volumes of descriptive properties and situations were published into books.

One thing that I do that goes one step further is to make a reference listing of characteristics. An encyclopedia of what and how people, and things, and animals, look, both in physical features, and also how they act, what they say, and how it is said; including the situations where they spoke and appeared at the time. This of course includes the characters emotional content of their personality in those various scenes, time of day, and associations with other characters in the scene.

I then try to categorize them into various features and expressions, places and situations. The clothing they were wearing at the moment, or if they were wearing any. I even have a category about the weather. What it was doing right then and if it made the scene more complicated.

All these get put into a dictionary of sorts, so when I need to find a particular type of character I can refer to this compilation. Type them up and print them out and then get a three-ring binder to hold all the wild and woolly, motley crew I have gathered with the knowledge I can grab all the items associated with what the particular character may have to offer.

Doing all this with knowing that I can change anything at a moments notice. This information is not etched in stone.

Okay, now how do you gather all this up and what do you do with it all ? The answer to this is probably oversimplified; you gather it all up from everywhere.

The easiest character sketch to start with is yourself. Sit down in front of a mirror or friends mirror, and look and observe the details, the nooks, and crannies of your face. Every feature of you is an important part of a potential novel or short story.

Remember every author puts a bit of themselves into their writing and their characters. And after you get used to looking at all your flaws and wrinkles, find the best way to put the details down in a detailed manner. Listing sketches in this fashion will be the only time you get to use adverbs to describe anything that has to do with your work, especially if you are writing for children.

After you go and take on the world on a park bench or even a restaurant seat, and stop, look, listen, smell, and if necessary, taste. But especially feel. Remember we are not talking just about humans. It could be a tree, grass, dogs, cat fur, and what have you.

After a while, you will construct so many sketch listings writing them will become second nature, and who knows, people might be asking you to use them as a character model.

Two of the best character sketch volumes were written and compiled by Mark Twain and H.G. Wells. Both of which are multi-volume issues.

John Steinbeck also wrote character sketches. Often, he wrote letters to the characters in stories as if they were real-life friends. These letters were also composed of the times when he experienced difficulties writing, who came to visit on a particular day and so on. He composed these letters for the characters in *East of Eden*, *The Grapes of Wrath* and others. Both are well worth studying for understanding the character building process. While only writing to these characters for a short time each morning, he was able to construct a robust and meaningful base for the actors of his story lines.

They thought out every characteristic, right down to the fingernail and voice type. After doing these sketches and the books had been published, it was clearly evident to the reader who these characters were and what role they played in the stories. It became as if they were human beings. It was as if the reader had met them in person, went to eat lunch, and held a conversation with them.

Personally, I think this is an excellent method to refine characters. I believe this approach to be far better than outlining. It will give the writer an opportunity to get to know their characters, almost in a live personal manner. Afterward, you could easily format and file the information of the characters for possible future use as aspects in other character development. You will find characters coming out of the walls.

Take an afternoon and sit in a favorite park. Take out a pad and pencil and begin to observe the surroundings, watch the people. Listen to the atmosphere around you. Take notice of the things people are saying, without appearing to be eavesdropping, of course.

Write! Look and observe! Listen! Then do the best you can to absorb all of it.

Use every sense in this situation and observe the day, the time of the sun, if it is a day of weather. Are there sirens going? Any birds flying? What games are any children playing in the park? What are people saying? Are they angry, or sad? Is anyone yelling? What about cheering? Are there any babies crying? What about the color of people's clothing? The listing outline includes shoes they are wearing, or are they barefoot? Shoes indicate a lot about a character.

Then there is hair. Whether or not the character has a full head of hair or the hair is thinning. For that matter, is your character bald or balding? What about the women and men of your story? It is the very same question and answer process. You ask yourself a question and you answer by observing.

Jot down everything you can as quick as you can, in short. Take it home and expand the findings. As a basic way to keep track of your observations, take each of the descriptions and categorize them into four columns. One for each of the character types, the Adult Male, the others for the Adult Female, the children both Boys and Girls.

Go over the writing pad you have and from your observations look at every single descriptive item and place each into the proper column. You will probably find many of the items will work in multiple columns and for many types of characters.

Don't forget their names. Characters are nothing without a name. An identifier to determine who they are and possibly where they came from. How to come up with names is not as easy as you might think.

Steven King is said to use the phone books of surrounding areas and area codes. Others use street names that go together, for instance, Debbie Lane, Gerald Place. Or, if you happen to see two cities together on a freeway sign, they can also be a useful resource for names. There are hundreds of ways.

There are digital tools that can include some simple utility apps that help writers with items such as name construction. The app developer Thinkamingo (Thinkamingo.com) has an entire product line of apps for writers. One called Name Dice is one that is a vital tool if you have trouble coming up with names on a regular basis and is fun to use. Another, a not only useful but brilliant app, is called Lists for Writers.
This app is the best utility for this function I have ever used.

Name construction and the part that takes time is figuring out if the chosen name for a character fits the attitude, the demeanor, and the look of the character overall.

Imagine yourself having a small and frail looking accountant type of gentleman. He carries a light brown, leather briefcase. He is always pushing his horn-rimmed glasses back up to the edge of his forehead.

A stereotypical character, isn't he? Do you understand the kind of person he is? What would you name him? You certainly would not give him a name that doesn't fit his character. Dirk comes to mind, but Dirk, as a name, tends to make a reader think of a handsome man, with hair flawlessly combed and parted, each tooth in his smile perfectly polished and aligned. His right eyebrow slightly raises when asked a question. He may be rugged and popular with the ladies.

It depends on the story and the manner in which you want the character to act in the story. But really, be thoughtful when crowning a character with a name that may not go well together. If it sounds like it does not make sense, you are probably correct. Name, compare and view each character's name. If the shoes don't fit together, don't try to wear them.

Henry Smithers, remember him from above. He is our accountant guy that holds tightly to his briefcase. Henry Smithers fits this character like a glove. For some awkward reason, we envision a bookkeeper type like this and the name Henry fits the bill nicely. It could be Gerald or Morty, a shortened version of Mortimer. That may be reaching a bit, but you have the idea.

When naming a character, time is not a factor. There is no rush. It does not need to be christened and kept right away.

You will change names off and on, and throughout an entire story. You will change names many times. How many names is determined by methodically and patiently fitting the name. You might say, "If the name fits wear it."

On the other hand, writers must never forget this very useful piece of information.

In the book written by Ernest Hemingway entitled *Death in the Afternoon,* he writes about characters as people.

*"When writing a novel a writer should create living people; people not characters. A character is a caricature.*

*If a writer can make people live there may be no great characters in this book, but it is possible that his book will remain as a whole; as an entity; as a novel.*

*If the people the writer is making, talk of old masters; of music; of modern painting; of letters; or of science, then they should talk of those subjects in the novel.*

*If they do not talk about the subjects and the writer makes them talk of them he's a faker, and if he talks about them himself to show how much he knows then he is showing off. No matter how good a phrase or simile he may have puts it in where it is not necessary or irreplaceable, he is spoiling his work for egotism.*

*Prose is architecture, not interior decoration, and the Baroque is over. For a writer to put his intellectual musings, which he might sell for a low price as essays, into the mouths of artificially constructed characters which are more remunerative when issued as people in the novel is good economics perhaps, but does not make literature.*

*People in a novel, not skillfully constructed characters,*

*must be projected from the writer's assimilated experience,
from his knowledge, from his head, from his heart, and from
all there is of him.*

*If he ever has luck as well as seriousness and gets them out
entirely they will have more than one dimension, and they
will last a long time."*

Hemingway was saying characters must not be merely a
character of one dimension. It is the writer's responsibility
to transform the one dimensional character into a three-
dimensional person. A character is a rough draft of an actor
in your story. The writer must write a real person for it to
become real to the reader. Polish the character and bring
them to life.

In a sense, it is as if Pinocchio has gone from a wooden boy
character to a real boy. The puppet is now the memorable,
breathing, laughing, active, heart-beating entity your readers
will not only share an emotional connection with, but one
they will keep in their memories. The writer has made the
character go from a flat, unfolded, cardboard box to one of
depth, full of demension, and containing life. That is what
readers expect and enjoy. They want to have a relationship
with your people. Not just be an acquaintance with someone
they will forget.

# Chapter 28 - Agents

Agents are wonderful people. They are busy, industrious, knowledgeable, and they are considered to be the gatekeepers to the publishing industry. They are underpaid, overworked for what they do for an author, and they do the heavy lifting for authors when it comes to the negotiations process. Something authors are not skilled in doing. They are knowledgeable, connected, and they're some of the most personable people you will ever meet.

They are also the liaison of the author, the go-between representative from Publisher and Writer.

They are the good folks who know how to negotiate the good deals and then if the opportunity arises, the great ones. They keep track of when royalty payments are due, and they are always in the background, making sure everything continues to be a win-win for everyone involved with a book project.

They pick up the pieces when things seem to fall apart. They decipher contracts. They are honest with you about your work (at least the legitimate ones are). They are there to say a friendly Hello, from clients they already have. And they know what they are doing, despite what suspicions your new writer mind may think it knows about agents.

Agents are passionate about writing. These are the specialists in the industry who can instantly tell when a manuscript has potential or not, and if it does, are able to know what publisher may be interested. Agents are the ones who can tell a mile away when a manuscript is crap and yet still have the diplomacy to tell the author they are not interested in representing it.

These are real people.

Most of all, they are unsurpassed in their knowledge of the publishing industry and for what is selling therein.

That is why they are agents. Being gatekeepers to the front doors of publishing firms has been placed in their hands along with the duty of making sure only high-quality manuscripts go forward to their appointed rounds on the desk of an editor.

It is the job of an agent to make sure no interlopers make their way into the world of quality publishing. Agents are a blessing to those writers who want to be considered quality authors. It is this process of filtering the chaff from the wheat which separates the almost good enough from the great. It is those that publishers want and need to publish.

Most new authors have no idea why agents seem like they are harsh individuals whose only goal is to stop an author's manuscript, albeit wonderful in the eyes of everyone who has already seen it. If you didn't catch the previous paragraph, read it again. If you did not get the part about good enough and great manuscripts, you might need to read this chapter again.

When an agent is queried and asked to review a work for representation, it means one of two things regarding the work. The author's query work is professionally prepared, or it is not. It is that simple.

Andrea Hurst of the Andrea Hurst Literary Agency said this about queries:

*"You get only one chance to make an impression when you submit to an agent or editor. Your query letter must stand above the rest and show off your writing skills, and your manuscript must be as close to publication-ready as possible. This means there should be nothing unpolished about your work when it arrives in a submission in-box. And, it must be coming to the right agent that fits with your work and in the right format as requested on the agent's website."*

Part of the agent's profession is to be able to tell what is workable, marketable, and what is ready to pitch. Publishers ask agents to do this on a daily basis. That is why most major publishing houses will not accept for submission any manuscript that isn't represented by a literary agent.

It helps the editors recognize work that has been done by a professional; an author who knows the dance and what steps to dance. It helps the publishing process by saving time, and it gives confidence to the editor reviewing the work for possible production.

Always consider the steps you have completed before querying an agent. Has the work been edited by a pro? Is the work a first draft? I hope it is not. If it is, that is a quick route to the rejection pile. Never submit a first draft, EVER.

One of the deadly thinking patterns for an author is, "My work is perfect and does not need rewriting or editing."

Learn this now. No one is that good.

With very few exceptions, even a second or third draft should never be considered for submission. Wait and rework it a million times if need be. Remember to be patient with yourself and your work. If you are not happy with your work, then no one else will be either. Get assistance and make sure it is the best it can be.

Time is not your enemy. It is a blessing, and you should be grateful for it. It will give you the needed space to perfect the work. No one said it had to be turned in on Friday, as you might have done in school. I have read new authors and handed back work, and I could tell it was not ready for primetime. Again, you get one chance to impress the agent, be sure you don't pitch until you are ready. It is the most common mistake authors make.

If you have never been published by a traditional house and have tried to be, you may want to think about your writing experience, attitude, and mindset. Perhaps you have not learned quite yet how to write as a professional. You would need more practice on your craft. Or, maybe you will be stuck on the rock face we spoke of earlier, all because you did not take the time to learn, or felt you did not need to find out how to do the proper steps to the publishing dance.

Perhaps you have forgotten something, whatever that might be. That is up to you to figure out, or better yet, get professional assistance with your query letter and manuscript.

Another of the possible reasons you can fail at getting an agent to represent you is the lack of knowledge in writing a proper query letter. Query letters are the introductions of yourself as an author and your work. Agents will not tolerate a bad query letter. They do not have the time to read them all the way through. They can tell from the first two lines what it will be like. Your hook needs to be spot on or count on getting a *Thanks, But No Thanks* reply letter or email.

How do you write a great query letter? To write one is a long process and it takes time to do properly. You will write and re-write (sound familiar?). Polish and refine.

If done correctly, you will have done a piece of writing that is pretty close to perfect. It must be impressive. It will shine and sparkle, and everything in it will be a reflection of your writing and you. Refining your work is another part you must do on your own.
Agents will not do this for you.

Finding out stuff is part of what writers do.

Why do you think you need an agent?

Most people believe this only because they have been told they do, and most of the time by others who don't have an agent. Strange thought, but it happens a lot.

The new writer has always been told that to get anywhere in the publishing world you must obtain a literary agent for representation of your work. What the new writer needs to do is concentrate on writing their work to an excellent polish. Learn everything you can about writing, learn the industry. Read the trade magazines online and in hard copy. Take classes and go to writer conferences. Most of all, practice writing every day and never stop. Learn how to know the difference between just good writing and great writing.

Right now, as a new writer, it is probably a waste of your time trying to get an agent at this time in your career.

This is why.

There are many business items most writers do not take into consideration. The professional aspects of book publishing. These are critical when the business side of the agent's world kicks in.

It goes like this. Do you have a track record? How long have you been out and about in the author world? What have you done to make your brand happen? How many books do you have in print?

Or are you not published yet? Have you queried an agent with nothing but a mere proposal of an idea and no written book to show for it? Or you have no sales to speak of and have no sales figures to show as testimony to how well your work has done or is doing?

Yes, these are all things to think about if you have just started. You need to work hard and get the word out and sell. If you have a hard time speaking to people and cannot promote yourself and your work, pack up your kit bag and smile, then politely walk away. Do not waste an agent's time or your own, attempting to get their valuable attention.

But what if I write in one genre? Do agents represent one genre or different ones for the same writer?

Yes and no. The difference between an agent that handles one genre or many is something the agent needs to decide. There are all types of agents. Some specialize in non-fiction, fiction, children's and young adult, and many others. There are agents who handle all genres. Check their website and such excellent books as: *Jeff Herman's Guide to Book Publishers, Editors & Literary Agents.*
Also join www.publishersmarketplace.com and research agents there.

Regarding sales and percentages, for domestic sales agents get paid little, about 15% per sales deal. If they use a foreign rights agent, the commission is usually about 20%. This comes out of the author's sales figures, royalty sales, whatever.

This is based on what the representation contract indicates between the author and the agent. Subsidiary rights such as book club sales, audio, etc. are generally included in the agent/author contract.

It has been this way for years, and it does not look like it is going to be changing anytime soon.

There are times when a new author should ask questions of a potential agent and should not feel intimidated. This is an important relationship you are entering into.

However, be sure to see if most of the answers that may be asked are already (and they usually are) included in the submissions information on the agent's website, or they may be in the Literary Agents Market Place listings published by *Writers Digest*, and several other publications. As a new author, you should be checking them all, to be sure the information coordinates with all the resources you have researched.

If all the information is the same, then you can be sure it is accurate. First and foremost, with any agency, be certain you have looked at the section where it states if they are taking submissions and double check the agent's website for CURRENT information. Logic dictates, if they are not taking submissions do not send one.

One of the most talked-about issues I get asked on a regular basis are about rejection letters. Personally, I think the term rejection letter is not correct in its title. Since the term is not a reflection on anything personal, or whether or not your work is shot down the garbage slide, someone should begin to call these dreaded letters something else. To be rejected is often held as a term towards a persons well being. Not as a business response.

Publishing is a business after all, and that is all it is. Not a psychological evaluation on you as a writer or how you think or write. Agents are not out to make anyone feel like crap. They are trying to find that one of a kind manuscript that they think that has a chance of getting published. Agents face a lot of rejection too, and if they have signed an author and put all their time, energy, and enthusiasm into selling it and it is declined by publishers, it impacts them as well. They perform many hours of work often for little or nothing at all. and Yes, they too get rejected by publishing houses. They are there to represent you and your work. They are on your team and are not just in it for the money. They are there to help you become successful.

Disappointment is a part of this business, unfortunately. It happens to the best of us. Just remember to breathe and re-evaluate, and then study what might have been made better and make a strategy for what your next step is. Take your ego and put it in your pocket and keep it there. Blaming an agent does not make the path easier and delays taking responsibility for what really needs to be done. It is you the writer that all the responisbility rests. No one else.

On this topic, Andrea Hurst and Sean Fletcher from Andrea Hurst Literary Management stated in a recent article for *Writers Digest Magazine* entitled *Look Before You Leap* published in October 2016.

WHAT THE AGENT SAYS:
Sorry, but this isn't for us.
WHAT IT MIGHT MEAN: It very well may be a subjective judgment—or just not a good fit for what the agency. Decisions like this often reflect market concerns: They may think this area of your genre is saturated. Occasional vague rejections can be inevitable, but you can minimize them by being sure you tailor your submissions to agents' most current guidelines.

Agents will continue to be an important part of this literary world, and I doubt they will be disappearing any time soon. They can make all the difference in the success of your book and writing career.

So, go to writer's conferences, meet some agents, editors, and maybe even publishers. Talk with them, get to know them as people and let them get to know you, as much as time allows. Don't just talk shop (unless they want to); they do that all day long every day of their lives. They are human beings and not someone who you may have placed atop a pedestal. They believe in what they are doing as much as you do. Connecting with an agent, if it works out for you, is a win-win.

*Special thanks to Andrea Hurst and Sean Fletcher of the Andrea Hurst Agency. www.andreahurst.com*
*Andrea Hurst has more than 25 years' experience in the publishing business as a literary agent, freelance developmental editor and bestselling Amazon author. Sean Fletcher works with Andrea Hurst & Associates as an agent, scout, and editor.*

# Chapter 29 - The Imagination

**W**hen children are little, the imaginations they possess disable them slightly. They are not able to see proportion or scale when their wild-eyed imaginations are in gear.

Kids see the world so much larger than it is. Children can look at a small lizard of four or five inches and after a short time will go running off to their mom or dad describing a monster in their back yard of five stories tall. Only they can tell if it is friendly or not.

The child's imagination is the most dominant force in the world today. With this tool, they have the ability to transform a simple cardboard box into a thousand-room castle, to create or destroy entire galaxies, to invent and discover cures for the incurable, and to bring forth world peace in the afternoon.

We as adults need to try to re-energize the imaginations we once had as children. We have allowed our minds to become as rusted old tools, left out in the rain, becoming wet and degrading. Perhaps our minds have lost their sharpness and polish, and so they have become hard to use in their present condition. I find that sad.

If that is the case, then it is time to take our imaginations to the sharpening stone and hone them back to the level of polish and sharpness that we once possessed as young people. It is important that we at least try to keep our minds in shape. Anyone who does creative work knows they must maintain their tools in the best condition they know how.

It is those who have been able to keep that finely sharpened edge on their imaginations that become the writers, inventors, creators and dreamers, and the helpers of humanity.

Because, without the childlike imagination that we are all given when we were small, the world would be a gray and lifeless place. We must find a way to be sure all our imaginations can be kept in fine working order.

How we do that is a personal thing. To maintain a creative, imaginative ability takes time and practice with an ability to put to a kind of discipline using imagination on an everyday basis. To find the time is real control. Anything practiced must consistently be exercised for at least a few minutes daily. The imagination is a powerful gift. It presents to all who use theirs, a method of transforming and rejuvenating life in a way that can only be brought forward through writing ( in this case), using the construction of story structure and plot.

I am sure there are other methods of making this work, but for now, we will explore this.

The human mind is a vast horizon made up of many things; it is impossible to comprehend the number. The creative side of the mind is one of the infinite. So much so that no one can dare to discover exactly how many. So massive in fact, there is no mathematical method to determine its size or capability.

The abilities of the human mind are endless. Science has barely scratched anything we can call a surface. When it comes to being used as a tool for writing, it increases exponentially.
We do not know its size or power.

Studies have told us our powers of mental ability are tiny compared to what scientists say we may be able to do if we had full capabilities.

Our imaginations are colorful. They are packed with a palette of every known color possibly known to man. There is so much more we have not discovered, only because we have not seen them with our eyes, they are not known to the imagination.

When writers begin to use this most valuable of creative tools, more so than a computer or pencil, they start a revolution of creative wonder that is endless. It will go on for eternity if the writer wants it.
Unfriendly worlds can erupt before the eyes of the reader; small children can become heroes. The most unlikely of

characters become something entirely unexpected while saving an entire universe.

A mouse can bring joy and laughter to a house cat; ghosts can come to visit a curmudgeonly and miserly old man on Christmas Eve, or a giant gorilla escapes and runs amuck in New York City only to find his demise over the love of a human girl. The worlds are endless on the roads of the imagination.

The beauty of imagination is exquisite. It welcomes the writer gently into realms never explored and never dreamed and beckons the words onto paper to pull a reader into the fantasy. Without pain or regret, the imagination brings to the writer an ability to do the same for the reader.

The practice is easy. It is the discipline which is difficult. Find the time to place words to paper and to make lists of places, characters, how someone speaks, what clothing they wear, how tall they are, where they live and the region they live. What kind of situations they find themselves. Bring them all together, and the puzzle begins to form and grow into something worth reading.

The imagination is a blessing. It brings together ways to invent, to inspire, and to provide many things to our lives. Our imaginations are endless. The number does not exist that can be graphed to illustrate the light years of possibilities we have. The imagination is the one completely awesome item we use daily. Without thinking, we bring to the front of our minds the ideas and concepts all of us share whether we know we are creating or not.

The onslaught of items and new invention which we live. with all began with someone's imagination. It shall always be that way as long as humankind can process thought.

# Chapter 30 - Creative Writing Class

There are schools not capable of bringing forth the writer in you. It is not for doing good work in English class, but plain and simple inexperience when it comes to the myth that everyone is a good writer.
Here is the reason.

Not all teachers have the experience in a creative writing atmosphere or can even attempt to bring that mindset into the classroom for the students. So they, in all essence, are not qualified to teach creative writing. It is rare that you find a teacher that is published or has industry experience.

It is necessary to practice daily, techniques and methodologies to learn the grammar and structure it takes to become a good primary writer. That is the only aspect of a creative writing class that carries any credence. These classes do not make you an actual author.

Please bear in mind not all teachers are guilty of this. However, in high schools and colleges I have found this to be true more times than not.

Creative writing instructors (I will be nice here) usually do not have a clue what the term creative writing means. Just because someone has an English degree does not mean they are qualified to produce quality writing or have any experience in the publishing industry. This does not hold true for all of them. So be aware. I am not blasting anyone here.

For example, they may not know what the terms voice or writing style mean. These are vital to a writer in how they discover one's writing voice and how they craft one's writing style.

In my opinion, these instructors do an injustice to the student who comes to them with good and innocent intentions to learn more about the writing process, not just mechanicals of writing periods and commas.

Quality writing is what most students are hoping to create in class. Everything from writing exercises in style and technique to the processes and habits the great authors who came before us used. The student must learn to question why these authors wrote the way they did. How come they generated sentences in the fashion they did? What was the purpose of placing the punctuation where they did (other than the standard period or quotation marks)?

Simple creative writing in its most primitive form is the primary effort spent in dumping words onto paper without any professional finality. Creative writing in its true form is the mere enjoyment of writing words without the stress or need to have them published for professional monetary gain. That is perfectly okay to do. I often write something with the full knowledge I will not be trying to get it published.

Creative writing is fun, and I have no problem with that if that is what it is. Your imagination can be let go to explore where it wants to go. Most of the time many of these creative writing classes have you write something for an assignment for a week or so. Then you bring it to class, and you take your turn reading what you wrote to the class. Then the class usually tells you that was the best thing they ever heard without any helpful critical review of the work.

It is a time in class where anyone who can place ink on paper can say they are a writer. The class is a great place to have your ego stroked. It is the task of the teacher to give a grade for what you finished. I have no idea how anyone can give a grade based on a class run by student ego.

Personally, I stay away from creative writing courses in high schools or colleges. I do not need the amateur critique. Rarely have I ever found one that is worth its salt. To get a formidable and realistic critique, give your work the gift of being reviewed by a professional writer or editor. Not by someone who claims they are a writer, yet has never published in any form.

In the chapter entitled *Never Let Your Mother Read Your Work* I state for one simple reason; mom is not qualified to give you a reasonable critique. Neither are the classmates in a creative writing class. Since they are not professionals, it is really the blind leading the blind. You can always depend on Mom to tell you that your work is at least nice. Each can only say what they felt was good or sounded good.

I am known in writing classes (creative) at a university I was asked to attend as a guest. I was invited by the instructor and the students to be ruthless in my critiques. However, my reputation preceded me. Once the class knew I was coming to listen and read their work. No one showed up.

I am not the evil ogre I have been known to be.
I am constructively honest, not malicious when it comes to a piece someone has asked me to critique. If anyone is considering the idea of getting published for real, as the writer, they should know that in the real world of publishing, things can and often do get pretty rough. Because of that, they should know what to expect and how to deal with it. I would expect the same from any of my editors or reviewers when it comes to my work.

Being accountable is okay. It is not a failure. It is only an opinion. Not the diabolical finality of what you are as a person or writer. Just something to think about. That's it. Nothing else.

In an earlier chapter, I mentioned I was asked by a student to listen to what they wrote, and then tell them what I thought of their work. I listened, and I told them. They burst into tears. I was critical, but not harsh. I told them it was scattered and it needed a lot of re-write.

They could not take that. They answered, "It had been re-written over, and over and the words were as good as they could be."

They were not prepared to have someone tell them the truth about their writing. As I stated, just because you can write and have the ability to place words on paper, does not mean you know what you are doing.

Seldom do I have an instance where I viciously tear apart anyone's writing, unless they want me to. Rarely do I verbally rip a work apart. But I have, if only to express to the writer (notice I did not say author) that perhaps maybe they should be doing something else.

Creative writing is an excellent practice method. It is a way to find something that resembles your beginning voice for your work and you as a writer. It is a way to know if you really want to become a professionally published author, or if you have the stomach to be one. Some find they do not. But most of all, it is a fun way to express yourself and share your thoughts to all who may be interested.

Be aware of the creative classes which come in the guise of a simple get together of people who know nothing other than words in a sentence and being nice to one another by complimenting what might be work not worth the ink with which it was written.

By all means, keep writing. Perhaps there will come a time when a light goes on, and an epiphany comes to the forefront, and then you can say, "Yes! I can do this."

## Chapter 31 -

## First Giraffes and Rough Giraffes

When beginning a new work for the first time and spilling it all onto a piece of paper, I consider what it is I am dumping and how fast I need to do it. Is it an idea I am just getting out of my head so I don't lose it, or something a bit more substantial? At any rate I still need to get it out of my head and onto paper somehow. I can then determine later if it is worth continuing.

I have, in the past, vomited an idea onto a page, as Ernest Hemingway suggested, and then realized it was garbage. But, more often than not, I have done it with intent so deliberate, the piece had no choice but to be held accountable and made to first draft status.

First drafts for me are an important part of my process when I write.

If anything I do makes it to, as a little first grader friend said, "A first giraffe," then I know I will continue with it. He then asked, "How many giraffes does it take to make a story?" I told him as many as want to come along for the ride.

We are taught in school, unfortunately, that we need to get things done fast, and as immediately as possible by the sheer lack of time. Many curriculums insist on this.

Let's say you get an assignment on Monday and need to have it done before Friday to hand in. Now, there is nothing wrong with deadlines. However, to write anything well and as complete as possible, takes time. It also takes many more drafts than we ever expect.

How many? It takes as many as it takes to complete the task. Seldom can a good work happen in such a short time as a week. It is often the case in schools. It's hard to teach that real-time writing is a fantastic kingdom where time holds no bounds. It is a severe task–master when it wants to be. That is most of the time.

First drafts are just that, a draft. A draft is an incomplete account or beginning of a piece of work. Drafts are then polished and need constant revision. They demand it. Changes occur so often they will make a new writer want to quit.

Why?

Because they are stuck in the idea they have written the great novel everyone will read. Not so. Never so. The new writer will hopefully, at some point, realize that writing is hard work. There have been works of my own that I have revised so many times I thought I would never get them finished.

A revision is an act of creativity in which the writer will make the work better until it is easy to read, easily read out loud, and will be easy to tell someone about. A revision is a part of writing which asks the reader not to trip over words and sentences. If, while reading the work, the writer still finds it clumsy, they need to re-write again.

But how do you know? How will you know when a piece is complete? It will tell you. It will tell you by saying and showing you that no matter how many times you correct a word or rewrite a sentence, it was better the other way round. Okay, so, you put it away for a time. Whatever that time is, is up to the writer. Two weeks is usually a pretty good span of time. Then go back to read and re-read it, and if it sounds fine, be happy, it is complete, at least for now. If not, then you have more work to do.

Drafts are and always will be, the marble in which a writer sculpts the writing. Chipping and carving away at the medium they use to bring forth a work all the world can like or turn away in disgust. It takes time, or as the great children's author Roald Dahl wrote in his excellent book Willie Wonka and the Chocolate Factory, "It takes a long time to put a million pieces together."

It is those million pieces that are the puzzle you need to look after. You must be sure no parts are missing before, during, and afterward.

Rewriting is part of the craft of writing. It is a must do thing. Don't be lazy.

In the beginning of your writers journey, be sure to plan, map out, and outline, everything you can think of when writing your first rough. Then do it again and again if need be. The more planning you do, the better the writing will be. After a time, you may abandon the outlining method, but during these beginning years, and yes, it may take years, you need to stick with the planning technique in everything you write.

First and foremost, get the words on paper, and if the words make no sense, that's okay. You have at least begun.

# Chapter 32 -

# The Two Sides of Self-Publishing

Since the advent of the self-publishing phenomenon, the publishing industry has taken strides surpassing any time in its history. The self-publishing industry in itself has developed and grown in ways traditional publishing never could. The technologies, methodologies, and overall long-standing trend have become a standard and an almost state-of-the-art technique to get books produced.

Business models for these have arrived, had great success, and some have grown to immense proportion. Not only is this business model one for soft cover, hard copy book production, but one for the digital book or e -book world as well. The e-book trend is no longer a trend but a standard, and it appears it will be sticking around for some time. Though it is only a small percentage (4% at the time of publication) of what the world knows as publishing, it is a sector that has been a constant since its arrival on the publishing scene.

Both types of book publishing have their methods, and with those, there also comes both good and bad aspects. The madness to all of this is still that it takes a long time to write anything worthwhile and sellable.

It will be a long time coming before any book is efficiently produced. But if you look at this from the perspective of how production people and editors see books as a whole, it will never reach a speed of less time than a minimum of 12 to 18 months to have a well-produced publication, even if you self-publish correctly. The editing still takes lots of time. And when edited accurately, it may take even longer.

From the editor, the work will go to the layout people, and they make their magic happen. From there, the work will go to the printer and bindery, then the packer and shipper and wholesaler and distributor and then to the store, and finally if it makes it, to the advertisers.

No matter what type of book it is, it all takes time and lots of it.

But time is a small thing to wait on in comparison when looking at the other things a new writer should learn when it comes to getting a book production completed, and it has become a full-fledged production.
There are many to consider and learn.

First off, if a new writer has never asked questions of themselves or their work, it is about time they did. It is an issue long over-due for new writers.

Most writers in the world have something they wish to share. It could be an experience they may have had or some knowledge regarding something or perhaps someone; these are all to be shared in the eyes of a new writer.

So, let's look at things in this fashion. Imagine this- you are standing at the base of a high rock wall. It is a sheer, straight up and down, granite wall, and you need to get to the top to get the best view of the world.

What do you do?
Do you start climbing?
How do you do it?

Are there any tools or techniques you need to know before starting up? Or do you, as in many cases, have within you enough arrogant confidence, you just begin to climb, only to find yourself stuck after having only reached four feet off the ground.

You are asking what have I done? You have reached a time that will either (if you have any common sense) tell you to go learn how to achieve your goal or one that will (if you do not have any sense) get you into trouble time and again.

This decision is yours.
Providing you opt for the common sense approach, it will take you much longer to reach your goal, but you will reach

it and without much difficulty.

However, if you just start up without knowing what you are doing, you will never reach it. You will become frustrated and fed up and wonder why you ever made this decision. You will be stuck somewhere on that rock face not being able to progress in either direction, not going anywhere. You will have failed and will be looking foolish at the same time.

The publishing industry does not suffer fools. It looks for quality manuscripts. It wants well-edited, well-written works that follow plot with relatable characters which are easy to read.

Publishers want to be able to be happy with what they are about to produce and advertise, and not some half-baked work that was slam dunked by a so-called writer who thought they knew everything about the craft of writing. If you have ever wondered why a publisher did not accept your work, think about the rock face.

You will find this far more apparent in e-books because they look easier to produce. They are not. There is far more technology going on in an e-book. The training and coding techniques it takes to learn to produce an e-book is intense. Yes, there are applications that can make it easier, but the coding within those applications is what makes it so. These are not perfect.

You will find sections of lines not formatting correctly, or not being able to place any graphics within a story. Will the title line or chapter line stay put when placed on the page? If not, how do you fix the issue?

Most e-books are text only. If you are a children's writer and are working with illustrations, it is much harder to produce an e-book.

Then to the wonderful extreme, if you are trying to create an interactive e-book for children, and you want to build it yourself. Forget it. You will need to take college courses to get your book completed. That will mean more time and more money. That will mean if you cost out your book when all your overhead is included, you will have priced your book out of the marketplace, making it far too expensive to purchase.

But wait! Do you have to learn all this technology to produce a book or an e-book?

No, you don't. If you look at this self-publishing gig as an easy way to get a book done, look again. Here's what the real world will tell you. It does not matter if you are trying to produce a printed book or a digital book. Companies such as Create Space® and a few others may produce a digital book for a small fee. You just need to work with them to be sure they have not changed any text, made sure your graphics, if there are any, are in the right place and so on.

One of the main issues with e-books is how is your book going to be seen? What type of format are you producing it for? Is it Mobi or EPUB? What kind of reader will it work with when you hire a company to build your book? What are the contract stipulations? You need to be sure it all works, and you need to be confident in the person or

company that is producing the e-book.
Give yourself an education in the world of e-book construction and research companies who can do the job for a reasonable cost and find out what their track record is for building an attractive and readable digital book.

Let me explian the difference between the terms Self-Publishing and the Independent Publishing. Self publishing is simple in that you are doing everything. You are publishing your project yourself. Thereby making it necessary to know everything about how to publish your work.

Independent Publishing is where the Publisher ( you) knows enough to know that you know nothing, and so you need to bring on those who know how to get things done. Making it easier on you by not needing to know everything. You still will need to know quite a bit, just not everything.

For the self publisher - to start, you have complete control. In reality, all that means is you are entirely responsible for the project. This is a scary thought. You must also know how to do everything regarding the project.

It means monetarily, as well as everything regarding production decisions. You must know what an ISBN number is and how to get one or several. Have you talked with someone at your county busines licensing board and registered a publisher name? You cannot get an ISBN without a publishing name. Have you paid the fees they want? Have you paid for an individual LCCN number? Do you know what a BISAC category is and how to get one ? Do you know how to obtain your copyright, or where to get the work formatted before it goes to press? Do you know what a press is and what that process is? What a press check is if you can get one. What font do you want the work to be done in and if your choice is licensed for commercial usage by the font creator? And just as an added item, have you scheduled an appointment for a consultation with a copyright attorney to get it right the first time? Very pricey by the way. What about proofs and PDF copies? What about getting a bar code for your book? E-books and hard copy books require them if they are to be sold on the open market at stores, distributors, and wholesalers. Which type will you need? Will you remember to figure in all the production costs which include these items mentioned above?

Why do you need to know all this?

*Reminder–this is not, by any means, all of it.*

Simple, if you do not, you might as well have never done the project. Without the information listed here and documented by you, the author, anyone can effortlessly take your work and claim it for themselves, and there is nothing you can do about it. It is important to document the project every step of the way, so this is never allowed to happen. Now, there is a certain amount of trust involved with self- publishing.

Of course, you would not be operating a press and many of the other technical things that go into producing a book. You must depend on the people who are skilled and trained in those operations. But because you have learned what they are doing, you will be empowered enough to gain more confidence in how your book is being handled. The trust you need to place in the people who produce books daily is essential to your sanity. Otherwise, you will become a nervous wreck wondering if everything is going correctly.

Self-publishing is just that, in every meaning of the word, you are acting as the publisher yourself. You wanted full control, and so you have it, to a point. The point is when your work goes to press or editing and other parts of the process, it is vital you know the steps and jargon of the process. If you do not, you may be setting yourself up to fail.

Self-publishing is a wonderful method for those who can stand to stick with it and do it in a step-by-step systematic methodical, fashion. Make a list of the steps and check them off as you complete them. There is a ton of work involved. A self-publisher needs to do all the work and needs to know how to do the work. A writer who will work hard to do everything as correctly as possible. They are the people who will not be afraid to ask the needed questions to do the project as it should be done.

Doing things correctly takes time as stated earlier, but understanding what that time asks for is a blessing. One which will continually reward both the writer and the reader. Correctly completing a project is the best and only way. Nothing should be otherwise.

A correctly processed project in self-publishing can elevate your name as an author, it can help gain prestige for you as well as the work, and it can be the make-or-break decision for an editor. It will also generate sales and elevate the author's notoriety, thereby bringing more sales. When you think about it, it is a beautiful chain of events.

So why would you want to do a project any other way?

The main negative in writing a book and producing it yourself is your attitude and the outpouring of money it bleeds. Remember the cliff climber that wanted just to get to the top and not learn what to do beforehand? Their attitude was what got that writer into trouble. A good positive mindset is the one thing that will save you when the writing needs it. But if money is something that is in short supply, then it may be you need to find another way.

Self-publishing has a long and reputable history. It is the method of publishing with which many of the most famous authors produced their work. Either by subscription or by a literary patron or just using the money from their coffers. All of it was expensive for their era. The other black cloud over the self-publishing model is what are called vanity presses.

These are the companies that promise the world and do little to obtain it, and at the same time charge you your left leg for the result which is usually close to nothing at all.

Companies like this still exist. They are completely legitimate and legal, but they have given a bad and sour taste to the publishing industry, and have covered many self-published authors with a dark, and negative stigma. This domino factor caused other authors to be stereotyped with an air of being less than legitimate, with the applied thought from the publishing industry that a real professional would never have gotten into a situation like that. An amateur forever will you be in the eyes of the traditional publishing world. That is the way it used to be. Not so much now.

In today's publishing world that stigma no longer holds due to the numerous writers who have taken the plunge to get their work into book form. But there is a negative aspect to all this.

The world of Self-Publishing has not only drawn out some splendid writers, but it has also brought out the dreadful, bringing the real crap out. Good, hard working, would-be authors need to avoid this type of garbage writing. The term garbage in, garbage out applies here. The acronym may be familiar to you. If you place garbage in your work, it will look like garbage in the end result. Namely your book.

Agents and editors both say this is the leading cause of rejected and trashed manuscripts. The incredible lack of care and understanding of the way a manuscript should be submitted, not to mention the amount of arrogance in a new writer when it comes to submitting a manuscript as a first draft finished, demeans the efforts of all those who are sincere in getting their work published.

Having to take the time to look at someone's work who has obviously not cared enough to follow the steps of submission guidelines for the house where they want to be accepted, is number one on the pet peeve list for most editors and agents. So if you have ever wondered why your work was rejected, think about it.

The time it takes to complete a manuscript correctly, get it edited appropriately and then submitted correctly is worth every second if you decide to self-publish.

Be it traditional publishing or self-publishing, both business models take time, and both need to be done correctly every step of the way. As a writer and would-be author of a book it is up to you and your knowledge or lack of that determines it all.

The publishing industry will continue to rally on for some time. It will not wait on you.

Do not lose your patience or drive to learn, nor your patience for yourself and your work.

Every writer who is interested in self-publishing should learn everything they can before taking the plunge or get left behind at the bottom of that rock wall.

# Chapter 33 -

# Some Do's and Don'ts

When a person decides to take on the marvelous, mystical world of sitting down and writing thoughts, they have entered into the world of the reclusive writer. At least it appears that way. The only real reason they work alone is that they need to be. It is out of necessity they write and create by themselves.

To be alone with thoughts and ideas is the most important aspect of being a writer. No interruptions. No distractions. No phone calls or dogs barking, and no kids yelling or spouse or partner wanting something.

A writer's life, what they have of it, is one which must not be disturbed. They are not rude or anti-social, they just need to get something done, and this is the only way to do it.

Much of the time writers hone their craft in the wee hours after everyone has gone to sleep. Often, when the kids are at school, or the house is quiet, the writer takes advantage of silence, and creates then. Some, if they live in a busy city, have the privilege of being able to listen to everything around them, gathering and collecting all the information that echoes from the city streets or surrounding areas. Here, there is no shortage of writing opportunities and material.

They can find a gentle, quiet corner. The writer locks themselves away in a room where no one has access to them while they are working. It's okay, the gremlins around you will get used to the idea that you are working and are not to be disturbed. Now is your time, your space, and you are not to be bothered. When you get into the writer mode, you will not even want to know when dinner is ready. I cannot tell you how many meals I have lost out on, only because I only had another sentence to write.

The idea is, when first beginning to write anything, is to start with the first words. If they do not make sense at this point, so what? You are on your way.

Do it again and again until you have what you were going for, or until you run out of words for the time being. Take a rest and come back to it. Your eyes will thank you and your mind will thank you. It is much easier to take a time out from work and come back to it, than to slam dunk it into what will, in the end, result in a frustrating jumble. Do not try to put it all down in one session. Not the best way to write.

No matter how good you think it is.
Think being the defining word here.

Do not self-edit as you write. It is dangerous and a waste of valuable time. As with any draft, get the words onto paper and clean it up later. Don't try to fix your writing while you write. It is for this reason editors exist. Let a good professional editor do their job, and you will have a far better work for the effort.

Do the best you can to remind yourself to write in text format or a familiar word processing application. I suggest the text size of 12 points because it is a clean, and more often than any, a clear, easy to read format. It is also transferable to any application that uses a word processing platform. You can use the old stand by typewriter if you want. However, watch for the mistakes that many writers miss. Mistyped words, words that are not completely legible (only partially black and are faded). Never use white out, or overuse erasers. They smudge the typing paper and in the end, make a tragedy of the work. So perhaps a typewriter is not a good idea.

When writers start out, they often scribble out the idea, just to get it down on paper and then go to the computer to flesh it out. Never the other way around. Number one on the list is never send a handwritten manuscript to any publishing firm's editors. They have no time to decipher your chicken scratchings.

If your goal is to be published by a traditional publishing house, then learn who the editors are. Misspell an editor's name and forget your chances of being published by that firm.

The best way is to do some research. Use the Marketplace books. They usually come out a few times a year and have tons of information on current editors, their names, and what it is they are in charge of, and in what departments they work. It is easy to send a manuscript to the wrong editor in a publishing company. It can get lost in a large loop and never been seen by human eyes ever again. Either by accident or a careless author sending work to the incorrect department, your manuscript has just entered no man's land.

If your research in the Marketplace books has lead you to the area and genre in which you are writing, now do some research and see if your findings match what is on the internet for the publishing house you are querying. If they do, then your chances increase of getting your manuscript checked out by an entry level editor.( To review see chapter 17)

Writing groups and clubs are valuable assets to the career of a writer or would-be writer. Find one or two that work for you and join them. Attend the meetings on a regular basis. Talk with members. Learn everything you can about all you can. The more you know, the more professional you will appear in the eyes of an editor. Just keep in mind that editors are people too, and their goal is to hunt for that potential best seller.

Now find your spot and start writing.
What do I write, you ask?

Close your eyes and breathe. Open your eyes when relaxed and then bring the words out into the world.

# Chapter 34 -
# The Dos and Nevers of Writing
# for Publication

**D**o this before anything else. Before you put any words down on paper and before you start to think about any aspect of writing, any genre for publication, evaluate why you feel you want to be an author. Is it for fun to see if you can do this, or are you serious about it. Writing will take a ton of work you may not be expecting. Are you willing to sacrifice? With writing, there are many things and people you may be giving up. It is a hard thing to figure out.

Are you a hobbyist, or are you willing to put your all into this demanding career? Most new writers or those who would like to see if they can get something published are doing this wonderful journey for the wrong reasons. It is not an easy road to travel and it is filled by the stragglers who have come before and failed or they simply gave up. This will help you keep going.

*Do #1-*

Always strive for perfection. At least as perfect as can be. Remember this: Perfection is a term too often used as a description for writing of any sort.

Rewrites are important. Never think your work doesn't need them. Re-writes are the polish the words and sentences need to solidify them. To make them as close to flawless as you can get them. Think of a rewrite as the preparation of a child going to school for the first time. You are making sure they are healthy, hair combed, their teeth brushed, and they know how to speak to an adult. When submitting work, run down a list of all the details. The work is proofed and edited by professionals. The work is ready for the real world in the hope it will be accepted to become published.

*Never #1-*

Never accept less in yourself or your writing. Don't be lazy and do not let your work look like it is lazy. Your words should be something that represents you, and it should most of all be clear in what it is saying. If you do not, you will appear amateur. A non-prepared, impatient, attitude filled, pseudo writer any editor will spot a mile off.

---

*Never let your ego or your emotions get in the way. It can ruin things quickly. There are reminders throughout.*

---

*Do #2-*

Be passionate about your work and what you are writing. The more passion you have, the more emotional power you will place into the imaginations of your audience and the passion will show through. In itself, it will make you a better writer. You will make the reading experience a real event. In the case of non-fiction an easier effort to achieve. Find one area you know well and write about it. It is a great place to start. Write what you know, and you will always succeed.

*Never #2-*
Never write something less than you know you can do, or should be doing. Expand your process and thoughts. If you need to research something, do it. Never be lazy.

---

*"Avoid writing something just because it is down and dirty, and is the latest trend. Trends do not last long. Be better! Be a visionary!"*

---

*Do # 3-*
Change your thinking for the better. Your attitude will make or break you and your writing career.
Remember, attitude determines altitude.

*Never #3-*
Never let your ego loose. As a writer, that would be like chasing chickens around a barnyard. If you have never chased a chicken, try it, and you will understand. It is a necessary evil, but worth having, if you can control it. The ego is a blessing and a curse for many new writers.
It causes difficulties where the writer becomes too much of themselves and becomes wrapped up in the absurd world of the elitist writers. Remain humble.

Never think a first draft is perfect. First drafts are never perfect; not even close. First drafts will be re-written on average no less than 20 times through the life of a manuscript. That may only be in one chapter or sentence.

Be patient with your work. It is inevitable it will need re-working, and therefore the evolution of the piece will take time. Do not be in a hurry. If you are, the work will look and read like crap.

*Do #4-*

Read, study, and take apart every piece of writing you can stand to read. Read things you would not otherwise read. Books, magazines, articles about topics you have never read before and items you never would have read. They are all valuable to your style and voice. Especially any and all classic literature. They will teach you why and what the authors of those times wrote. It will possibly take you to the thought process of the author and help you see inside their mind.

Remember, it is the classical authors that broke ground for us in the modern world.

*Never #4-*

During the first draft- stop thinking. What? You must drop the words onto the page without any thought or process of them making any sense whatsoever. That will be cleaned up at a later time. Thinking is not writing.
Never be satisfied with your first work. Knowing you have a great story is a powerful thing. Every great author has done this.

They have polished every word and paragraph to an excellent shine. Make the work brilliant.

*Do #5-*
When it comes to writing, with the exception of a children's fiction work, do the research on the topic first. Mystery writers are always on the prowl for the information they need to make a story feasible, and truer to life.

When it comes to submissions of manuscripts, be sure to check all guidelines, addresses of the primary company address and any imprints, double check listings of current editors for the firm you are submitting. Be sure to spell the editor's name correctly. Use the internet and read the market listings.

Contact publishers with a physical letter and not an email. You will get better results this way. Unless, of course, in their guidelines they require email only. Request their current book titles listings for every company they have. Publishers may or may not send it to you. They will ask if you can nail down which imprint interests you.

It saves them money. The list might be sent via email. If publishers have a titles listing, request it via snail mail. Be sure to place your current email information in your cleanly typed and printed letter. Include a paid envelope as well.

When you get the listing, study it. Ask yourself, why are particular titles included? Would yours fit into their listing?

*Never #5-*
Don't check just one resource. Each large publisher has several different listings in many different market publications. Make sure you are contacting the proper editor, and double check to see if that editor is still with the publishing house. Remember laziness is not acceptable. Take the time to do this correctly.

The research will cost some money if you purchase all the market books. Pick your genre and find the market book appropriate for your goal.

*Do #6-*
Common and logical sense is a factor in this.
Would you sell your apples to an orange dealer? No, of course not. The orange dealer will not buy the apples. Be sure to know what imprint is buying what topic before sending yours out.

*Never #6-*
Never forget your writing project is now called a product. The publishing industry looks at it that way.

*Do #7-*
Do EVERYTHING each set of publishing guidelines tells you to. Do the very best you can to stick to them in detail and to the letter. Remember, each publishing house is going to have a different set of guidelines. There are no two the same.

*Never #7-*
Never send your work for submission if you are stressing and losing sleep. That is a sign you are not ready.

Relax and breathe. Be patient with your work and yourself.

*Do #8–*
Hire a reputable professional editor. Yes, it will cost some bucks.

*Never #8–*
Never stay at a writing group or writing association or club if it is not constructively critical. Don't keep attending if it makes you feel uncomfortable. Attending a bad one will not help your writing or your confidence.

*Do #9–*
Find a writing mentor. Someone who is in business and has been for some time. Be sure they are willing to help you with questions and an occasional critique if they have time. Their time can become expensive. They may charge for their time and experience. So ask ahead of time.
Never assume they will work for free. Remember you get what you pay for.

*Never #9–*
Don't feel they will help you on your schedule. To a mentor, the word *immediately* does not exist. Their schedule dictates their lives.

*Do #10–*
Take a refresher course in English grammar, or journalism. It will show you new techniques in writing.

*Never #10–*
Never take a course on writing for publication from anyone that has not had at least two books published, or has not been at all.

That is like having surgery done by a blind person.

*Do #11-*

Change your mindset. Just because you think your work is great does not mean anyone else will. The publishing industry is business first and something that appreciates books and great stories a close second. Ask yourself, how is your product going to sell in the marketplace? Research it as much as you can.

*Never #11-*

Don't assume that because you wrote a story on horses, that a publisher that has published horse books in the past will still be producing books on horses. Double check the titles listing again. Remember those?
Do your market research. Yes, it takes time, but what else do you have right now?

*Do #12-*

Practice writing every day. Write every day for at least 30 minutes. It is not a ton of time. You will find it to be too short. If that becomes the case, then, by all means, write for a longer amount of time. The more you write, the better you will become.

Set a time you can sit alone and write for yourself and stick to it as best you can. But, as it is said, "Life happens!" You cannot avoid it sometimes. When it does go with it and let the flow happen.

*Never #12-*

Never edit on a first draft. Just write the thing.

The first draft will always suck. There is nothing you can do about it.
Don't sweat it if a first draft is not perfect. It is what it is.
Don't sweat it if you are not writing correctly.

Ernest Hemingway said this about first drafts.

*"Vomit the words onto the page and worry about cleaning the mess later."*

Good advice.

*Do # 13-*
Do the best you can to write timely stories. They are the ones that stand against time and enjoyed for generations. Thousands of readers will continually appreciate these books.

Stay away from trends. They are temporary and fleeting, and usually, by the time you have written your piece, your trend is long gone, and so is all the blood, sweat, and tears you once wrote, that much better.

*Never #13-*
Never write about little sponge characters who live beneath the sea, or write about farting dogs or square kitchen tools that come to life. They have been written about to death. You want better. You want the best you can do. Go after them. You have better stories that will come to you.

*Do #14-*
Work hard. Write your best work. Never be satisfied with mediocre.

*Never #14–*
Let anyone discourage you.
Never pay attention to the word no.
Lose heart.
Be sloppy

Do #15–
Be patient with yourself and your writing.
And then write some more. It does get easier.

Do these  especially –

Learn the rules of the industry, and then break those rules
without it looking like you did. .
Let your renegade come out.
Be brave enough to be different.

# About the Author

T.E.Watson is a veteran of the publishing industry of some 43 years. His knowledge of everything from children's books and young adult to various non- fiction works is well known the world over. He is now venturing into the realm of the murder mystery genre. Quite a switch according to him.

With some twenty-two literary awards and two Author of the Year awards for 2001 and 2009, he is asked many questions on the subject of publishing and becoming published.

He has compiled many of the questions he has been asked over the years into *Light and Stone, Essays on Writing and the Realities of Publishing* in hopes he will be successful in helping new writers as well as those more experienced gain more knowledge of the world of publishing.

He is a columnist, writing and book consultant, and speaker. His audiences vary from community organizations to schools, seminars, and has presented at writer conferences domestically and in Europe.

He lives in Northern California with his wife and three cats. (And other wildlife who come to visit.)
For more information, you may contact him at -
tew@tewatsononline.com
Or at his web site – www.tewatsononline.com

52179872R00141

Made in the USA
San Bernardino, CA
13 August 2017